ISBN 978-1-331-36229-6
PIBN 10179502

1 MONTH OF
FREE
READING

at
www.ForgottenBooks.com

By purchasing this book you are eligible for one month membership to ForgottenBooks.com, giving you unlimited access to our entire collection of over 1,000,000 titles via our web site and mobile apps.

To claim your free month visit:
www.forgottenbooks.com/free179502

Abraham Lincoln in 1861

From a photograph by Hesler, in possession of F. A. Brown

ABRAHAM LINCOLN

BY

WILBUR F. GORDY

AUTHOR OF "STORIES OF EARLY AMERICAN HISTORY," "STORIES OF LATER AMERICAN HISTORY,"
"AMERICAN LEADERS AND HEROES," "AMERICAN BEGINNINGS IN EUROPE," "COLONIAL
DAYS," "AMERICAN EXPLORERS," "ELEMENTARY HISTORY OF THE UNITED
STATES," "A HISTORY OF THE UNITED STATES FOR SCHOOLS"

"Let us have faith that right makes might; and in
that faith let us, to the end, dare to do our duty
as we understand it."—LINCOLN.

CHARLES SCRIBNER'S SONS
NEW YORK   BOSTON   CHICAGO

PREFACE

IT is an old and true maxim which says that we learn from experience; meaning, of course, our own personal experience. But much is to be learned also from the experience of others, especially of the great and the good who have lived before us. Herein lies the value of biography. By coming to know, through books, men of great and strong character, we learn from their lives much that is helpful in living our own. For if in imagination we enter into their purposes and plans, their sorrows and joys, their defeats and victories, we learn through their experiences, and they become in a real sense our teachers, guides, and friends.

Perhaps to Abraham Lincoln, more than to any other man in the history of our country, has been given the power of influence over the lives of those unknown to him. To thousands who never saw him, but who know him through his letters and speeches, and through the record of his private and public life, he is an inspiration. The story of his overcoming the difficulties of his early life has put courage into many a young heart; his resolute stand by what he thought to be right has helped countless souls to be true to their duty; and the kindliness and good-will which flowed from his great heart toward all—even his foes—

CONTENTS

ILLUSTRATIONS

ABRAHAM LINCOLN

CHAPTER I

BOYHOOD DAYS

In the pioneer country of Kentucky, not so very long before that wild, wooded region became a State, began the life of one of our nation's great men. There, in a remote settlement on Nolin Creek, about fifty miles south of where Louisville now stands, Abraham Lincoln was born. Nothing in his surroundings or his early living conditions foreshadowed the greatness of the man or of his career. Possibly the natural simplicity of his life favored the growth of a great soul. Certainly none of the hampering conditions of luxury, or even of too comfortable living, held it back.

The immediate family into which the hero of our story was born was small, there being only his father, Thomas Lincoln, his mother, Nancy Hanks Lincoln, and a little sister, Sarah, two years old. But there were many bearing the names of Lincoln and of Hanks in the country. Their ancestry ran back to the early beginnings of New England, and the names themselves were ancient English.

With the prosperous and successful branches of the

family we have little to do. Abraham Lincoln himself in
his later years knew little of them, not even of his grand-
father. He said: "I am more concerned to know what
his grandson will be." Knowing, therefore, that among
Lincoln's ancestors there were able and distinguished men,
we may pass over their achievements, and begin the story
of Abraham Lincoln's life with a brief account of his father.

Thomas Lincoln was the youngest of a family of five
children who were made fatherless by the shot of a stealthy
Indian when little Thomas was only ten years old. From
that time he was set adrift, "a wandering, laboring boy,"
to make his own way in the world. Yet at twenty-five he
had bought a farm in Hardin County, Kentucky, and had
learned a trade, being called "a good carpenter for those
days." So he could not have been altogether idle and
shiftless, though history has usually pictured him so. Besides, he was honest and sober, with strong common sense,
and was considered by his neighbors good-natured and
obliging; and his love of fun and good stories, traits he
handed on, made him unusually good company.

These qualities, even though he lacked thrift and ambition, won him the affection of the devoted woman who
became Abraham's mother. She is described as "sweet-
tempered and beautiful . . . the centre of all the country
merrymaking," and "a famous spinner and housewife."
She was the niece of Joseph Hanks, in whose shop Thomas
Lincoln had learned the carpenter's trade. She was

twenty-three years old at the time of her marriage, five years younger than her husband, but superior to him in appearance and in intellect, and in her ability to read and write; for until his wife taught him after their marriage Thomas Lincoln had never learned—possibly because he

Cabin at Nolin Creek Where Abraham Lincoln Was Born

had been thrown upon the world so young, or perhaps because he had no liking for books. Indeed, few of their friends could boast this accomplishment.

It was on June 12, 1806, that Thomas Lincoln and Nancy Hanks were married in Elizabethtown, Kentucky. The young couple began their housekeeping in a one-room cabin, fourteen feet square, like many others in Elizabethtown; and there in the following year their first child, Sarah, was born.

As Thomas did not have enough work as a carpenter to supply the growing needs of his family, he removed to the little farm situated on Nolin Creek, which he had bought three years before. Here, on February 12, 1809, Abraham Lincoln was born. Life was already an up-hill struggle for the Lincolns, and they soon became very poor. This was largely because the farm alone did not yield a living, and the father did not get sufficient extra employment at his trade. He would turn off work if it came his way, but he did not go to seek it.

After a losing struggle on the farm at Nolin Creek Thomas Lincoln, when little Abe was four years old, sold out and bought another farm of two hundred and eighty-three acres on Knob Creek, about fifteen miles to the northeast, and removed his family to that place. We may imagine that the journey thither through the leafy woods must have been a delight to the four-year-old boy, who was not old enough to be weighed down by care and disappointment. The song-birds, the flitting squirrels, the flowers, the sunshine, the wind, the trembling leaves and bowing trees, or even the cloud and storm, might well give joy to his sensitive little soul.

They lived on the new farm only three years, little Abe being seven years old when they moved away; but after he had grown to manhood, Lincoln could recall incidents of his life at Knob Creek. Here a baby sister was born and died. Here the little fellow began manfully to share the family work, fetching and carrying for his father, picking berries, even helping to plant seed.

But the family fortunes did not pick up; and as a dispute arose about the deed of his farm, Thomas Lincoln once more decided to sell out and seek a new home.

Most of the good land in Kentucky was being rapidly settled, and a good farm there would have cost more than he was able to pay. Moreover, a brother had prospered in Indiana, and other relatives had gone there. Then, too, as his son said later, he wished to go where there were fewer slaveholders. So this time Thomas Lincoln decided to leave Kentucky and cross into Indiana.

Of the first seven years of Abraham Lincoln's life we know almost nothing. His only playmate was his sister, Sarah, for neighbors were not close enough to see much of each other. He must have played much alone in the forest and about the streams, making friends with the world of out-of-doors. He was seldom known to speak of those early years even to his best friends, but when some one asked him later in his life if he remembered anything about the War of 1812, he told the following story: "I had been fishing one day and caught a little fish, which I was taking home. I met a soldier in the road, and, having always been told at home that we must be good to the soldiers, I gave him my fish." This shows us that as a child he was generous, and that he had been taught to be patriotic. Another of his memories was of his mother taking himself and Sarah to say good-by to the grave of his little sister before going far away to their new home in Indiana.

Thomas Lincoln sold his claim to the farm in Kentucky for twenty dollars and four hundred gallons of whiskey. Whiskey to us seems a strange kind of currency; but it was far less bulky than the corn from which it was made, and as trading was mostly by barter, or exchange, it often passed from one owner to another in the process of buying and selling.

With the proceeds of his sale and his kit of tools, he boarded a rude raft of his own making and drifted down the creek to the Ohio River, landing some miles below on the farther shore. Here he made acquaintance with a settler by the name of Posey, and leaving his whiskey and kit of tools with him, pushed inland through the dense forests in search of a suitable spot for his new home. On the first day he selected a place near Little Pigeon Creek, eighteen miles north of the river, and one and one-half miles from Gentryville. Then he walked back to Knob Creek for his family. Again the simple preparations to move were made, and the life in Kentucky came to an end.

Two borrowed horses carried their household goods, which consisted of a little bedding and clothing and also a few cooking utensils. The children were tied to the load upon the horses' backs. The father and mother walked, the father carrying his rifle to protect the family and provide necessary food. He carried his axe also, that constant companion of the pioneer, not only in the woods for chopping a way through, but at the journey's end for making the home and its rude furniture.

On reaching the Ohio River the horses were set free and headed homeward. A boat carried the Lincolns across the river, and on the other side a wagon was hired from Posey. Then Thomas Lincoln with his family started on their journey northward. As he had to cut a road through the forest, they were three days on the way.

The four were entirely alone. They had not even a domestic animal—a cat or a dog—with them. The journey must have been a dreary one, for it was the last of November and the weather was more or less wintry. They had no shelter at night except the leafless trees, nor any protection from the cold except the clothing they wore and the brush fires around which they slept under the open sky. Yet the two children probably had much pleasure out of the changing experience.

Having arrived safely at the end of their journey, all set to work with a will to provide a shelter against the winter. Young Abe, though only seven, was healthy, rugged, and active, and all day long he worked with his axe, clearing away the bushes and thick underbush, while his father cut down saplings and made poles for their "camp."

This "camp," in which they must live until they could build a good cabin, was a mere shed, fourteen feet square, with one side open. The poles were laid one upon the

other, and were topped by a thatched roof of boughs and
leaves. As there was no chimney there could be no fire

Lincoln Helping His Father Make "Camp"

inside, and it was necessary to keep one burning all the
time just in front of the "camp."

During this first winter in the wild woods of Indiana
the little boy must have lived a very busy life. Besides the
building of the cabin, which was to take the place of the

"camp," a clearing had to be made for the corn-planting of the coming spring.

A whole year passed before the Lincoln family moved into the newly built log cabin, giving up the "camp" to some friends, Mr. and Mrs. Sparrow, who had followed them from Kentucky. With the Sparrows lived Dennis Hanks, a young cousin of Mrs. Lincoln.

The new cabin had no windows and no floor except the bare earth. There was an opening on one side which was used as a doorway; but there was no door, nor was there so much as a deerskin to keep out the rain or the snow, or to give protection from the cold wind.

In this rough abode the furniture was scanty and of the rudest sort. The chairs were only three-legged stools, made by smoothing the flat side of a split log and putting sticks into holes bored underneath. The table was of the same simple kind, with four legs instead of three. The rude bedsteads in the corners of the cabin were made by sticking two poles into the logs at right angles to the walls, the outside corner, where the poles met, being supported by a crotched stick driven into the ground. Then boards were placed across the poles, making a framework upon which shucks and leaves were heaped, and over all were laid the skins of wild animals.

Abe's bed was a pile of dried leaves in a corner of the loft, and he reached it by climbing on pegs driven into the wall. In winter the cold winds whistled about his head, the snow sifted in through cracks, and even the drip of rain fell on his face. ·

The food was simple, but there usually was plenty of it. The Lincolns raised enough corn to supply the household,

A Pioneer's Home

the meal being made into "corn dodgers," roasted in the ashes, which was their every-day bread. Wheat was so hard to raise and so scarce that flour bread was reserved for Sunday mornings. The principal vegetable was the common white potato, and sometimes that was all the Lincolns had to eat. We get a flash of Abraham's humor and learn something of his father's religious habits from Abraham's remark to his father, who had just asked a blessing on a dish of roasted potatoes, that "they were mighty poor blessings." But, as a rule, there was an abundance of game, such as deer, bears, wild turkeys, ducks, and pheasants, many kinds of fish from the streams close by, and in summer wild fruits from the woods. These were so plentiful that they were dried for winter use.

It was easy to get game, for not far from the Lincoln cabin was a glade in which there were deer-licks. Waiting here one or two hours usually resulted in getting a shot at a deer, which would furnish food for a week, and also material for moccasins or shoes and breeches. But the cooking was rudely done, because there were few groceries and few cooking utensils. A simple but most useful article in every pioneer household was the gritter. It was a piece of flattened tin punched full of holes and nailed to a board. Many articles of food could be grated on it, and at times the housewife secured by this slow method enough corn-meal for bread.

When washing-day came, the clothes were taken down either to the flowing stream or to the watering-trough, which at that time was the closest approach to our modern set tubs. Indeed the backwoodsmen had to devise many contrivances to supply their lack of manufactured things. Thorns, for instance, were used for pins, bits of stone for buttons, while for a looking-glass a woman would scour a tin pan. As there was almost no money in circulation, people exchanged, or "bartered," for things they wished, one man paying maple-sugar for a marriage license, and another giving wolf-scalps! Candles were a luxury much of the time, and Abe, as we shall find later, spent many long winter evenings reading by the light of blazing logs in the rude fireplace.

Method of Grinding Corn

These were busy days for Abraham. As a small boy he did the numberless chores which come around with surprising frequency to the boy who lives on a farm. He also cut brush, chopped fire-wood, picked berries, and helped plough and plant. Although in his brief biography, written in the third person, he said that he did little hunting, he told the following story about his shooting a wild turkey:

"A few days before the completion of his eighth year, in the absence of his father, a flock of wild turkeys approached the new log cabin; and Abraham with a rifle-gun, standing inside, shot through a crack and killed one of them. He has never since pulled the trigger on any larger game."

While the boy kept busy with tasks about the farm and helping his father in the carpenter-shop, the simple, active life was making his body strong and wiry, and his muscles firm and hard.

As he grew he became a tall, slim, awkward boy, with very long legs and arms. His dress, like that of all pioneers, was picturesque and somewhat peculiar. He wore trousers and moccasins made of deerskin, and a shirt, which was often of homespun linsey-woolsey, but sometimes of deerskin. In winter his cap was of coonskin, while in summer he wore a rough, unshaped straw hat without a band. Probably this costume was very comfortable and well suited to the pioneer's life; but we are told that Abe's deerskin trousers, after getting wet, shrank until they became several inches too short for his long, lean legs. Then his jesting companions called him "long-shanks."

But the privations of these "pinching times," as Lincoln later called them, were as nothing compared to the grievous loss of his mother. The rough life of the forest and the exposure of the open cabin had weakened her naturally frail constitution. Besides, there was much malaria, and in 1818 a frightful pestilence, called "milk sickness," swept away a large part of the people in the little community near Pigeon Creek. Among those who died were Mr. and Mrs. Sparrow, who had occupied the "camp," and Abraham's mother.

She was the nine-year-old lad's dearest friend. They

were knit together by common traits that held them in closest sympathy and understanding. They had the same alertness of mind, the same sensitive feeling, and the same strain of sadness tingeing their natures. Before her death, in her final parting, she said to the boy sobbing at her bedside in his first great grief: "Abraham, I am going away from you, and you will never see me again. I know that you will always be good and kind to your sister and father. Try to live as I have taught you, and to love your Heavenly Father."

There was a long interval after her death and burial before a preacher came near enough this remote settlement for a funeral service to be held. But before a year had passed, it is said, the young boy sent a message to a Baptist preacher who had more than once been a guest of the Lincolns in their Kentucky home, and persuaded that good man to come more than a hundred miles to hold a service at his mother's grave. The oft-quoted remark, "All that I am or ever hope to be, I owe to my angel mother," reveals the abiding love in which he held her memory.

For a year the family was desolate. Then Thomas Lincoln went to Kentucky to seek another wife and mother for the bereaved home. There he married for his second wife, a widow, Sarah Bush Johnston, whom the family had known before leaving Kentucky, and who became a devoted friend to the motherless boy.

When Thomas Lincoln and his new bride came back to the Indiana home they brought a wagon loaded with furniture, for Mrs. Lincoln was well-to-do. There was a fine bureau, a clothes-press, and bedding and cooking utensils such as Abraham and his sister Sarah had never seen. Mrs. Lincoln brought with her three children of her own, two girls and a boy. There were also now in the household, with the Lincolns, Dennis Hanks, who had come to live with them after the Sparrows died, and a cousin from Kentucky, John Hanks. This made in all a family of nine in the little cabin—a lively household indeed for the new mother.

Sarah Bush Lincoln was energetic, thrifty, gentle, and intelligent. She had been accustomed to better things than she found in her new home, and she insisted that the log cabin should be supplied with a door, floor, and window. She also began to make the Lincoln children "look a little more human." In fact, she was a model stepmother.

It was fortunate for Abraham that she was bent upon having the children go to school. He was now ten years old, and he could not write. Although he had gone to school for a short time to two different teachers before leaving Kentucky, he knew little more than the letters of the alphabet.

There were no schoolhouses in southern Indiana in those days. Such buildings as they had were rough log cabins which had been used for homes, with earth floors and greased paper for windows. Desks were unknown, little benches made of split logs after the manner of the stools and tables in the Lincoln home being used instead. The teachers were men of limited education, who could teach only a little spelling, reading, writing, and ciphering.

During his last school-days, Abraham Lincoln had to walk daily a distance of four and one-half miles each way from his home, following no doubt at times the deer-path through the forest. His midday lunch was a "corn dodger," which he carried in his pocket. He went to school to three different teachers in Indiana; but his schooling, all told, lasted less than a year.

In spite of his meagre opportunities, however, the boy by his self-reliance, strong purpose, and good reading habits was acquiring the best sort of training for his future life. At his home there were no books except the Bible, and of course there were few to be had in that wild country from other homes. But whenever he heard of a book anywhere, far or near, he would go on foot to borrow it. Then he would pore over its contents until he had made every· thing between its covers a part of himself.

To a friend he once said: "I have read all the books I have ever heard of in the country for a circuit of fifty miles." In this way he came to know thoroughly "Æsop's Fables," "Robinson Crusoe," "Pilgrim's Progress," "The History of the United States," and Weems's "Life of

Washington"; and these were all books of the right kind.

His stepmother said of him: "He read everything he could lay his hands on; and when he came across a passage that struck him, he would write it down on boards, if he had no paper, and keep it before him until he could get paper. Then he would copy it, look at it, commit it to memory, and repeat it."

Dennis Hanks said: "When Abe and I returned to the house from work, he would go to the cupboard, snatch a piece of corn bread, take down a book, cock his legs up as high as his head, and read."

When night came he would find a seat in the corner by the fireside, or stretch out at length on the floor, and write or work out sums in arithmetic on a wooden shovel, using a charred stick for a pencil. When he had covered the shovel, he would shave off the surface and begin over again. He liked to read or study while lying down, and this habit clung to him throughout his life. It was his habit also to copy, either in his copy-book or in a note-book which he kept for the purpose, the selections he liked. He used a turkey-buzzard's quill for a pen, and the juice of a brier-root for a writing-fluid.

The books that he specially liked he read over and over again until he knew them almost by heart. One that he had borrowed was Weems's "Life of Washington." The first night he had it he took it to bed with him in the loft, reading until his candle gave out. Before going to sleep, he tucked the book in a crevice between the logs until daylight should come, and he could go on with his

He Would Work out Sums in Arithmetic on a Wooden Shovel

reading. Poor Abraham! During the night a hard rain beat in upon the book, soaking it through. With heavy heart he took it back to its owner, who required him to work three days to pay for it. Although Lincoln paid the price he resented the injustice, and later took his satisfaction by writing doggerel verse in which he ridiculed the farmer. Yet the book was worth to him all it cost, for it had a marked influence over his future.

Abraham Lincoln's hunger for books led him to devour anything that was printed, even the dictionary, which he read page by page. With absorbing interest, he studied it, evening after evening, until the twilight made it impossible for him to see. He never seemed to get enough. Even the Statutes of Indiana were grist for his mill, as the homely old saying has it. The book containing these also had the Declaration of Independence, the Constitution of the United States, and the Ordinance of 1787. Here was the beginning of his study of law, which was an important stepping-stone in his career.

Such a boy did not need to go to school, for, having learned to read and to think about what he read, he was his own best teacher. He learned by reading how other men had won success in life's struggle; and by copying the things he wished to remember he made them his own. While there was not much need for arithmetic in the backwoods, he knew that in the larger world outside it was useful. In a word, he soon came to realize that the man who knows has a great advantage over the man who does not know; and being ambitious, he strove to give himself the power of knowledge—that knowledge which helps a man make his way in the world.

As we have noted, his stepmother was very desirous that he should go to school and also have an opportunity to read books. His father, on the other hand, having never been to school himself, thought that for a boy like Abraham schooling was a waste of time and that books were useless. To him it was more important that Abe should be earning money to help the family to live. It was for this reason that Abraham was allowed to go to school but very few weeks at a time, and that at seventeen he was taken out of school altogether.

In fact, before he was seventeen his father had begun to hire him out to the neighbors to do farm-work, or whatever the neighbor wished to have him do. For this the father received twenty-five cents a day. At times Abraham and Sarah were both hired out to the more thrifty farmers in the community, Abraham as a field-hand and Sarah as an inside helper. While so employed, Abraham, when in the house, was always ready to lend a helping hand to the busy housewife, by making the fire, carrying water, or even tending the baby. It was by such simple and homely services that he won friends wherever he was, and was always in demand.

He was a good worker, but he could not always put his heart into his work. His interest was in other things. A neighbor said of him: "He worked for me, but he was always reading and thinking. He said to me one day that his father taught him to work, but he didn't teach him to love it." In fact, his thoughts were centred in other things than his daily labor. When his employer's day ended, Abraham's day began, because it was then that he took up his books. He read and wrote and ciphered all the time he had for himself. As a worker, however, he gave satisfaction, because he was so strong and so intelligent; and he was a good comrade, because he had so much good humor and told so many funny stories.

He Liked to Make Speeches, and Often Amused and Entertained His Friends

Besides being a good story-teller, he liked to make speeches; and by his efforts in this direction, often amused and entertained his friends. When the time for a resting spell from work came, Lincoln would stand upon a stump, or climb a fence, and make a speech, sometimes repeating in part, with some variations, a sermon he had heard from the lips of a travelling preacher. Sometimes he would use his powers of speechmaking in the midst of working-hours; and whenever he spoke he never failed to create a lively interest in his hearers, who would drop scythe or axe and gather around the young orator with genuine admiration. By delaying the work in this way, Abraham often caused his employers to think that his oratory was robbing them of their dues. But he was so good-natured about it all, and so popular among his fellow workers, that no farmer could easily complain.

Although there was much hard work in those days, we must not think of his early life as altogether one of drudgery and loneliness; for even in the backwoods, there were many simple good times to enjoy. In his own home, we may be sure, there was much fun and frolic. Thomas Lincoln himself, as we have said, was a good story-teller, and so was Dennis Hanks. There must have been cheery talk, therefore, around the fireside. Abraham also went fishing with the boys in the creek in the evening. He enjoyed swimming, and during the rests at noon he and the other boys wrestled and jumped and ran races.

After new families had come to the region there were many social gatherings in that backwoods community, and Abraham Lincoln liked to attend them all. They included horse-racing, fox-hunting, husking-bees, house-raisings, log-rollings, spelling-bees, and political gatherings, where there were speechmakings.

On all these occasions Lincoln was a favorite because

of his wit and humor, his rare gift of telling stories, and his practical jokes. He was such a good speller that in course of time he could spell down anybody at the spelling-bees. In fact, it is said that after a while it was decided not to let him spell at all, for there was nobody that could match him.

In his own home he seemed to be the leader, largely because of his cleverness and kindness. But perhaps one of the strongest reasons why he won and kept an undisputed leadership over his friends and associates was his giant stature and strength; for in a community like that, physical prowess was in itself leadership. He had attained his full growth and height when he was seventeen years of age, being at that time six feet four inches tall. Then, too, people were proud to be his companions, because of his superior knowledge and power as a public speaker. Besides, he was so just that he could be depended upon to settle fairly disagreements among his friends.

We must not think of him as a perfect boy. Of course, like all of us, he had his faults. He sometimes disagreed with his comrades, and sometimes the dispute was settled in a rough-and-tumble way that resulted usually in favor of Abraham, for he was a strong wrestler. After he had grown up he rarely met any one in those backwoods days that he could not easily overmatch. It was said that he once lifted and carried a chicken-house weighing six hundred pounds, and also that he could lift a barrel of whiskey and drink out of the bung-hole, although the narrator declared that Lincoln would not swallow the whiskey. Even though these stories may be exaggerated, they at least show the reputation he had for strength.

A Grocery-Store of the Primitive Days

Gentryville, the village near which Abraham lived, stood apart from the great world of thought and action. No lecturer ever made this little place a visit, and not even a circus came within reach of its inhabitants. It lived its own life, and the centre of that life was the grocery-store. Here the idlers loitered during the day, and the busy men joined them at night. Could you have entered Jones's grocery-store in the evening, you would have seen men reclining on the counter or sitting on kegs and barrels, listening perhaps to a funny story or perhaps to a speaker, at times Abraham Lincoln, who was taking part in the debate. With as much enthusiasm as if the fate of a nation depended upon the outcome, they discussed such questions as whether the Indian or the negro had received the worse treatment; whether fire or water is the more useful; whether the merits of the bee or of the ant are greater. We may smile at the simplicity of it all, but we must remember that it was at the grocery-stores in these primitive days in the backwoods that ideas were gained and public opinion formed.

The people were superstitious. They believed in dreams, signs, and omens. They would not begin a journey on Friday. If a dog crossed a hunter's path when he started out in the morning, the hunter would have an unsuccessful day unless he at once hooked together his two little fingers and pulled until the dog was out of sight. If a bird alighted in a window or a dog was heard baying at certain hours of the day, it was regarded as a sure sign that death or some other form of calamity would visit the household. Potatoes and other vegetables yielding their fruit under ground must be planted in the period when the moon was not full; but those bearing their fruit above ground must be planted in the full of the moon.

As there were no churches in those early days, there was little public worship. From time to time, but at long intervals, a travelling preacher would pass through a region. Then nearly all the people would go in large groups to the nearest meeting which he held. If a pioneer had a wagon, his whole family were carried in it, and this was thought of as real luxury. But when families had no wagons, the mothers rode on horseback, carrying the little children in their arms. The men walked, taking along their muskets to be ready to shoot any game they might be able to start up on the way.

On arriving at the place of meeting they all put into a common store the provisions they had brought, and in cheerful companionship ate together in true picnic fashion. If the weather was fair and warm the meeting was held in the shade of the trees; but if it was rainy or snowy the people sought the shelter of some vacant cabin.

When all was ready for the worship to begin, the preacher took off his coat as a suitable preparation for the energetic speaking which, according to the practice of those backwoods days, was fitting on such an occasion.

In all this primitive life of the home, and of the community, Abraham Lincoln took a faithful part. But his ideals were higher than those of the people with whom his lot was cast, and he longed to get out of that backwoods country into the great world beyond. The highway to it led through the Ohio and Mississippi Rivers down to New Orleans, but this highway was as yet closed to him.

It opened up ever so little when, at seventeen, he found

employment with James Taylor, a man living at the mouth of Anderson Creek where it joins the Ohio River. Abraham's principal business was the management of Mr. Taylor's ferry-boat, which plied across the creek and the Ohio River, and his wages were six dollars a month and board.

It was the custom of farmers living in Ohio, Indiana, and Illinois to collect the produce of their communities on flatboats, and float it down the river to New Orleans. Abraham's experience on the river, where such boats were continually passing, made him wish to try a venture of his own.

An opportunity came when he was nineteen years old, while he was working for Mr. Gentry, a leading man of that vicinity. A trading expedition was planned by his employer to go with a load of produce to New Orleans. Lincoln was to go along with Mr. Gentry's son and aid him in handling the boat and selling the cargo, and for his service he was to receive eight dollars a month and board.

They were gone three months on this trip, and did not return until some time in June, 1828.

During these months on the river Abraham must have learned much of the ways of the world, and have come more closely in touch with its life. The pioneers with their produce-laden rafts—the house-boats with mothers rocking and children playing on deck, perhaps the family washing flapping in the wind—the steamers with their city-bred passengers and the ferrymen plying back and forth—all these, to say nothing of the restless life of the brilliant city of New Orleans, were stirring scenes which must have quickened the thought and pulse of the ambitious young backwoodsman.

But after this glimpse of the world Lincoln was again shut in, and once more he took up the petty makeshifts of life in the backwoods.

CHAPTER II

LINCOLN AS A YOUNG MAN

AFTER thirteen years of baffling fortune in Indiana, Abraham's father, Thomas Lincoln, was no further ahead than when he went there. He could not make his farm pay. Besides, the place was unhealthful on account of "milk sickness," of which, as you will remember, Abraham's mother died. John Hanks had gone west into Illinois and sent back pleasing reports of the country, and now the young people in the Lincoln family wished to follow, because they felt that there was nothing to look forward to in Indiana, where they were, but hard work and poor living.

So, about the middle of February, 1830, Thomas Lincoln, with his family and the families of Dennis Hanks and Levi Hall, who had married his stepdaughters, started west to try again at making a home. Sarah, Abraham's sister, had died a few years before. They sold their land, cattle, and grain, and much of their furniture, so that a wagon drawn by four oxen carried all the household goods. There were thirteen in the party. Abraham drove the oxen. Mrs. Lincoln rode on the load, and her little grandchildren were stowed away among the goods. The others walked along beside the wagon as it slowly rumbled through the country. The wagon-wheels, without spokes, were simply rounded blocks of wood cut from an oak-tree, with holes in the centre for the axle.

It was a difficult journey. The roads were not like those of to-day, but only rough trails through the forest. Freezing during the night and thawing during the day, they were hard to travel over, and even the prairies were covered with mud. The numerous creeks and rivers had to be forded on foot by the men, for of course there were no bridges; and when the water was cold enough to be covered with thin ice this must have been very unpleasant. For two weeks they travelled in this way, with very little to protect them from the cold, either by day or night, no matter how stormy the weather.

Yet it would be hard to believe that Abraham's stout heart did not make light of the difficulties on the journey, or that his active mind did not find much to interest him. Little has come down to us about it, and yet we know from his own telling that they passed through Vincennes, where he saw a printing-press for the first time. That would naturally interest the book-loving young man. He mentioned also seeing a juggler performing sleight-of-hand tricks in a country village. The thrifty side of his nature is revealed by the fact that before starting out from Gentryville, he had invested all his savings, about thirty dollars, in notions and a few odd things, like knives and forks, to sell on the way. He wrote back after reaching

Decatur that he had sold them all and doubled his money.

About the first of March their journey came to an end, some ten miles west of Decatur, Illinois. There, on the

Lincoln's Family Moving into Illinois

banks of the Sangamon River, John Hanks had cut logs ready for the new cabin. It was a very simple affair, for there was no time to do what was not necessary.

Although Abraham was now twenty-one years of age, he remained to help his father get started in his new home.

He not only joined in building the cabin, but lent a hand
in clearing the new farm of fifteen acres, and in splitting
rails from the trunks of the tall walnuts of the forest to
fence it in. "These are, or are supposed to be," he said
in his short autobiography in 1860, "the rails about which
so much is being said just now, although these are far from
being the first or only rails ever made by Abraham." He
then stayed to help his father plant and harvest the first
crop of corn.

Life in Illinois was much like that in southern Indiana.
There was the usual log cabin, consisting of a single room
with the planted clearing around it. When a new settler
came into a community, those who had come first were
ready to help him build his cabin, but after that he had to
look out for his own simple wants. Every family had to
be self-supporting; that is, it provided its own food with hoe
and rifle, and made its own clothing, even hats and shoes.

For chopping down trees and for fashioning the simple
furniture they used, the axe was still the most important
tool. Abraham Lincoln said once that from·the time he
took it up to help his father clear away the brush, he never
let it go "till within his twenty-third year." He was a
famous chopper. Dennis Hanks said that if you heard
him without seeing him, you would think there were three
men chopping, the trees fell so fast.

There was a coarse and rude supply of food, as in
Indiana. Game of many kinds abounded in the forests.

After a while, when swine became numerous, bacon and hoe-cake were staple articles of diet. Tea was made out

He Worked More or Less at Odd Jobs in the Community, Mostly Splitting
Rails or Working on the Farm

of sassafras roots dug up in the woods. Buckskin clothing was becoming less common than when Abraham Lincoln was a boy, although it was even yet sometimes used to

make moccasins and hunting-shirts. As the pioneers had begun to grow flax and hemp and to get wool from their sheep, home-made garments became more usual, for the women of the household could spin, weave, and fashion garments, as in the older communities.

Having helped his father to settle in the new home, Abraham began to take thought for himself. One of his first transactions was to bargain for some new clothes. He agreed with Mrs. Nancy Miller to split four hundred rails for every yard of brown jeans needed to make him a pair of trousers. As he was tall—six feet four inches—three and one-half yards were required, and he had to split fourteen hundred fence-rails—a large amount of work to give for a pair of trousers. But brown jeans were hard to get, and Abraham paid the price cheerfully. Then he started out for himself.

During the first year he worked more or less at odd jobs in the community, mostly splitting rails or working on the farm. He still spent occasional nights at his father's house, and doubtless made him now and then gifts of money.

Two things commended him as a worker. The first was that he was strong; the second, that he was a likable young fellow. His good humor, his funny stories, his wit, and his skill as a debater all helped to make him popular in the new community. He seems not to have been always a diligent worker. But when he did work he did it so effectively that he was always wanted.

Everything went well during this first year in Illinois until about Christmas-time. Then a great snow-storm, lasting nearly two days, covered the ground three or four feet deep with snow. Hogs, cattle, and even horses perished from the intense cold or from hunger. The winter-wheat crops were entirely ruined. Many people died, some from exposure and some from hunger, for only in places would the crust on the snow bear a team, and none but the strongest men were able to go on foot for food.

Toward the end of the winter Lincoln met Mr. Offutt, a business man recently come to Decatur, who had some produce he wanted to send down to New Orleans. He needed two or three hands, and he engaged Abraham Lincoln, John Hanks, and John Johnston, Lincoln's step-brother. Each man was to receive fifty cents a day, and if the venture succeeded, twenty dollars cash in addition. To young men so little used to money this seemed large pay.

First, the flatboat had to be built, a task which took four or five weeks. So it was about the middle of April before they started down the Sangamon River. The journey was an eventful one. Before they were fairly launched Lincoln had to rescue two of the company from the rapids in the river. A few miles farther down they had another serious mishap. Just in front of the little village of New Salem, on the Sangamon River, the flatboat stranded upon a mill-dam. Nearly the whole village came out and

spent a good part of the day looking on, offering advice,
and making jokes at the expense of the wayfarers.

Just in Front of the Little Village of New Salem the Flatboat Stranded

Perhaps the figure most interesting to them was a tall,
raw-boned young man, with a battered hat, a threadbare
and patched coat, and a pair of homespun trousers, torn,
patched, and with almost half of one of the legs gone.

This was Abraham Lincoln. He was attentively preparing
a contrivance by which to unload the cargo and get the
boat off the dam, for, with its bow in the air and its stern
filling with water, both cargo and boat were in danger.
Lincoln succeeded in removing the cargo to another boat,
and then bored a hole in the part of the boat over the dam
and let out the water. Soon things were righted, and they
proceeded on their journey.

They had no further difficulty in floating down the
Sangamon, the Illinois, and the Mississippi, and they
reached New Orleans in May, 1831, where they remained
for a month. The city had become even more prosperous
since Lincoln's first visit, made with young Gentry three
years before. Commerce had greatly increased, and the
population was larger and more varied, there being people
of many nations. Both the city and the life were picturesque, with much to engage the attention of a stranger.
Here were seen the idle luxury of the rich, the wild, wicked
life of the poorer quarter, the pirates in the Gulf and river,
and the crowds of river boatmen, with boats so closely tied
that one could walk a mile over them without going ashore.
Lincoln's quick, young mind, stimulated by all that he saw,
must have carried away sharp impressions of many phases
of life, to be thought over later when he was back in
Illinois, especially that part of it which brought him in
contact with the evils of slavery.

The city at this time was full of slaves, and their number was constantly increasing. One of the saddest features of slavery was the slave-market. Here Lincoln saw, for the first time, men and women sold like animals. He saw negro slaves chained and whipped. Looking on at a slave-auction must have given him a great shock. While one slave after another was knocked down to the highest bidder, his indignation grew until at length he cried out: "Boys, let's get away from this. If I ever get a chance to hit that thing [meaning slavery], I will hit it hard." Little did any one imagine how great a blow he would strike some thirty years later.

After the month spent in New Orleans, which must have passed swiftly, the young men boarded a steamer in June and made their way up the Mississippi River to St. Louis. From this point Lincoln and Johnston tramped across Illinois to Thomas Lincoln's new home in Coles County, in the eastern part of the State. Thomas Lincoln had again migrated, for he found that chills and fever were almost as bad in his first home in Illinois as "milk sickness" had been in Indiana.

After remaining with his father and mother four or five weeks, Abraham bade them good-by and started out to begin a new venture for himself. Mr. Offutt, for whom he had sold produce in New Orleans, had so much faith in Lincoln that he wished the young man to manage a store for him in New Salem. As Abraham left his father's house that July day, all his simple belongings were tied in a cotton handkerchief and slung across his shoulder. It must have been with mingled feelings of regret and anticipation that he left home and turned his steps toward the world outside.

The little town of New Salem was perched high on a bluff overlooking the river, at a spot about twenty miles northwest of Springfield. The village never had more than fifteen or twenty log cabins, crude huts, some of which it had cost about ten dollars apiece to build. In this unpromising centre Offutt not only opened a store, but he leased a mill also, and put Lincoln in charge of both, believing he could do anything he set his hand to. But, as we shall see, to build up trade in a poor little place like New Salem was akin to removing mountains.

For an assistant Abraham was given a young man by the name of Greene, eighteen or nineteen years of age. He belonged to one of the best families in the community, and here began a lifelong friendship between these two young men.

Offutt's great admiration for his new manager caused him to boast that he knew more than any man in the United States, and that he could beat any man in New Salem, or in the country around New Salem, running, jumping, or "wrestling." Of course, Abraham could not prevent his employer from thus boasting of his virtues, but neither could he escape accounting for himself. The boasts so irritated a gang of rough young fellows who lived at Clary's Grove, about three miles from the village, that they challenged Lincoln to a wrestling-match with their leader, Jack Armstrong.

Lincoln did not wish to engage in such a match, but he could not well get out of it. Armstrong, who expected an easy victory, soon found that he had more than his match. It was impossible to throw Lincoln.

When the Clary's Grove gang saw how the match was going, they crowded in, and by kicking and tripping Lincoln they tried to throw him. His anger gave him the strength of a giant. Seizing Armstrong in his arms, he gripped him by the throat and shook him like a child. Then, with his back against the wall, he defied the whole crowd.

The fury of the youths changed quickly to admiration of the stranger's courage and skill, and no one of them was more cordial in showing it than Jack Armstrong himself. The friendship between these two became like that between brothers, reaching down even to the next generation; and many years later Abraham Lincoln, as we shall see, saved the life of Jack Armstrong's son.

This incident of the combat established Abraham Lincoln in the respect of the New Salem community. There was no question as to his popularity. The Clary's Grove boys counted him as the cleverest young stranger that had ever come into that part of the country; and a year later, when Lincoln was running for the legislature, he received every vote that was cast at Clary's Grove.

Lincoln's experience as storekeeper in New Salem brought out very prominently one of the fine qualities strongly marked throughout his whole life. This was his honesty, which was deeply ingrained in his nature. It was a trait that showed itself in his clear thought, his simple language, and his freedom from pretense, as well as in his common every-day acts. Two instances will show you how he came at this time to receive the name of "Honest Abe." When, one day, he discovered that a customer had paid him six cents too much, he walked three miles after nightfall to refund her the money. Another time, when he found he had given false measure, he was greatly distressed. A woman had bought a half-pound of tea just at closing time, and on coming to the store next morning Lincoln noticed, from the weights left on the scales, that he had given four ounces less than she had paid for. At once he closed the store and took the rest of the tea, wrapped up in a package, to the defrauded customer.

This story suggests that there were not many waiting customers at the grocery-store, or Lincoln could not have locked it up and gone to correct his mistake so promptly. It is true that he found himself having much leisure time, and he determined to apply himself to study.

Since leaving Indiana he had seen much of men and life, but had done little with books. So now was the time to read and study and know them better. He had observed that men of power were men who had knowledge; and,

while always very modest as to his own ability, he could not help knowing that he had certain qualities of leadership in common with them. The people in the backwoods community always looked up to him, and he was determined to increase his power for leadership by increasing his knowledge. So with serious intent he began to read and study books all he could.

He talked about the matter with Mentor Graham, the village schoolmaster, and Mr. Graham advised him to study English grammar. "Where can I get an English grammar?" asked Lincoln. Graham told him that there was a copy of Kirkham's English Grammar in a family about six miles away. Lincoln did not wait. Getting up from the breakfast-table, he at once walked six miles and back to get the much-prized book.

Then he settled down to master it. In his usual way, where books were concerned, he bent all his energy to complete the task. Night and day he pored over the pages of the book, until at the end of three or four weeks he knew all that he could learn from the rules of Kirkham's Grammar. Sometimes he would ask his friend Greene, of the grocery-store, to hold the book while he recited; and again, when he needed assistance, he would go to Mentor Graham, who had helped him to get the book.

In such an earnest and determined way did Abraham Lincoln improve his leisure time while he was acting as clerk in the grocery-store at New Salem. But in less than a year Mr. Offutt failed in business there, and then the studious young man had more time on his hands than ever. He used it all to good purpose, for he was so eager to learn that, whenever he heard of a book, he sought its owner, borrowed the book, and was not satisfied until he had made it a part of himself. This love for books, together with his inflexible purpose to make something of his life, marked Abraham out from all others in the community. The neighbors, recognizing his strong desire to improve himself, were eager to help him. Mentor Graham gave him instruction, the Greenes lent him books, and the cooper in New Salem village allowed him to burn shavings in his shop at night, for light to study by.

Another reason for his success in New Salem, as it had always been wherever he had lived, was his great kindness. He was always ready to help others. If a wagon mired in the crooked, muddy lane which was the only street in New Salem, he was among the first to offer his assistance. If a poor widow's wood-pile was low, he chopped wood for her. He sat by the bedside of the sick. He rocked the cradle for tired mothers. In truth, wherever there was an opportunity to reach out a helping hand, there was Abraham Lincoln with friendly sympathy and kindly service. Thus he made friends, and all who knew this young backwoodsman not only respected and admired him for his ability, but loved him for his tender heart and generous spirit.

CHAPTER III

LINCOLN A LEARNER IN THE SCHOOL OF EXPERIENCE

IT was during this period, when Lincoln had neither home nor regular work, that an opportunity came to him for a new experience.

One April morning, in 1832, the Governor's messenger rode into New Salem scattering circulars that created much excitement. They were addressed to the militia and announced that the Indian chief Black Hawk was on the war-path. They called for volunteers to meet at Beardstown within a week.

Early in March Lincoln had announced himself as candidate for the State legislature, the election to which would take place in the autumn. But he was one of the first to volunteer for the war. He and one other were rivals for the position of captain. The men voted by gathering, as their names were called, around the leader whom they chose, and three-fourths of them took their places about Lincoln. He said later that no success ever came to him which he appreciated so much.

The men were a motley-looking group, each being dressed and equipped as he saw fit. Many wore deerskin breeches, a few coonskin hats, and all had powder-horns thrown

44

over their shoulders. It was no easy task to govern them, because they had the pioneer spirit of doing pretty much

Selecting Lincoln as Captain

as they pleased; but this independence was out of place in the army, where every man must forget himself and take orders from his commanding officer.

As captain, Lincoln did not always know his duties. Among his many borrowed books there seems never to have been one on military rules and regulations. Between the waywardness of his men, therefore, and his own ignorance of military terms, his discipline was far from efficient. On one occasion his superior officer took away Lincoln's sword because he fired off a gun within the camp limits. On another occasion, when the soldiers stole some liquor at night and drank so much that they were unable to "fall in" the next morning, Captain Lincoln was humiliated by having to wear a wooden sword for two days.

His unfamiliarity with military terms brought about some humorous situations. One day his company was advancing across a field with a front of over twenty men, when they approached a narrow gateway, through which they would have to pass in single file. Lincoln had to give the order, but he did not know what to say. It was necessary to think quickly. Here is his own story of what he did: "I could not for the life of me remember the proper word for getting my company endwise, so that I could get it through the gate; so, as we came near, I shouted: 'This company is dismissed for two minutes, when it will fall in again on the other side of the gate!'"

But, in spite of his ignorance of military rules, his men admired him because of his physical strength, his good humor, and his ready wit. They cheerfully obeyed his commands because they liked him so much.

Lincoln saw no fighting, but he had opportunity to show his fearlessness by risking his life to save a helpless

Abraham Lincoln at About Thirty-five Years of Age.   From a Photograph after a Daguerreotype in Possession of Hon. Robert T. Lincoln

Indian who came to the camp one day bearing a pass from the commanding general. This Indian was a trusted friend of the white people. But Lincoln's men, not knowing him and fiercely hating all Indians, desired to kill him. They seized him and were about to shoot him when Lincoln declared that he should not be harmed. After vainly trying argument and persuasion, at the risk of his own life he placed himself between the rifles of his angry men and their victim, thus saving the Indian's life.

The war, which ended in the defeat of Black Hawk, was a short and uneventful one, and before fall Lincoln was back in New Salem, ready to plunge into the political campaign for election to the legislature. When he had announced himself as a candidate he issued the following statement: "Every man is said to have his peculiar ambition. Whether it be true or not, I can say for one that I have no other so great as that of being truly esteemed of my fellow men by rendering myself worthy of their esteem. How far," he added, "I shall succeed in gratifying this ambition is yet to be developed. I am young and unknown to many of you. I was born and have ever remained in the most humble walks of life, and if the good people in their wisdom shall see fit to keep me in the background, I have been too familiar with disappointment to be very much chagrined."

Although Lincoln received all but seven of the two hundred and eighty-four votes cast in his voting district—

which included the village of New Salem and the surrounding country—he was defeated in the election. This was especially disappointing as he was without either money or business. But in his brief military career, and his still briefer political campaign, he had broadened his experience, and was not content to take up again the dull routine of the ordinary day-laborer. Yet he had to do something to earn money enough to supply his simple wants. So for a time he took up odd jobs. Sometimes he would help in the corn-field, and at other times he would chop logs and split rails, build fences, or do whatever task, light or heavy, happened to come his way.

There were many places in New Salem where he was always welcome. Two of the homes where he went most often were those of Bolin Green and Jack Armstrong, the hero of Clary's Grove. Hannah Armstrong, Jack's wife, took pleasure in making him feel at home with the family. "Abe would come out to my house," she said, "drink milk, eat mush, corn bread and butter, bring the children candy, and rock the cradle while I got him something to eat. . . . He stayed at our house two or three days at a time."

Naturally, Lincoln's friends, since he had such uncertain means of support, gave him much advice as to what occupation he might best take up. On account of his great physical strength, one of them advised him to become a blacksmith. But he preferred an occupation which would give him more leisure for study and an opportunity to come into touch with the world of thought.

Having already tried storekeeping, he knew that this gave opportunity to meet the leading men in the community and discuss with them politics, religion, and other topics of interest, and at the same time tell to eager listeners the stories he enjoyed narrating. Besides, in the village where he had lived the storekeeper was a leading man. So he decided to take up storekeeping, and in the autumn of 1832 he and a man named Berry bought three grocery-stores in New Salem. Having nothing to pay, they gave their notes.

They appear not to have done a thriving business, but Lincoln turned his leisure to good account. Scouring the town and the entire community for books, he pored over their pages, even forgetting sometimes his waiting customers. It was no uncommon thing to find him sitting upon a wood-pile or lying on his back under the oak-tree just outside the store door, with his feet resting high above his head against the trunk, "grinding around with the shade." When his neighbors came and saw him reading in this position, many of them laughed and some thought he was losing his mind. But Lincoln knew what he was about. He was preparing himself for the larger, richer life he hoped to live.

It was during this period that a little incident occurred which, although apparently unimportant, changed the whole course of his life. It is better, perhaps, that we should hear the story in Lincoln's own words: "One day," he said, "a man who was migrating to the West drove up in front of my store in a wagon that contained his family and household plunder. He asked me if I would buy an old barrel for which he had no room in his wagon, and which he said contained nothing of special value. I did not want it, but to oblige him I bought it and paid him, I think, half a dollar for it. Without further examination I put it away in the cellar and forgot all about it. Some time after, in overhauling things, I came upon the barrel, and emptying it upon the floor to see what it contained, I found at the bottom of the rubbish a complete edition of Blackstone's 'Commentaries.'"

This book, as you may know, was once an authority in law. To Lincoln it was a true gold-mine. He had a natural bent for legal matters, and it awakened his deepest interest. He read it hour by hour and day by day, never wearying.

But this reading of law and other books did not help out his storekeeping. Neither partner was giving careful attention to the business: for, while Lincoln was studying, his partner Berry, who was a gambler and drinker, spent much of his time in the back of the store, where the liquor was kept. A business which runs itself cannot be expected to run long, and the storekeeping venture did not prosper.

But, fortunately for Lincoln, in the spring of 1833 he was appointed postmaster. Although the mails were scant, the new position helped out a little. Twice a week the mails were supposed to come, but many times there was none for two weeks or even for a longer period. Lincoln carried the letters in the crown of his hat and delivered the mail to the people as he met them, or took it out to their houses, some of them at a considerable distance, as the community was a scattered one. It was his privilege as postmaster to read all the newspapers that came to the post-office; and he could usually tell the recipient, in advance, all that the newspaper contained. Perhaps this opportunity to read the newspapers was the perquisite which most strongly appealed to Lincoln when he accepted the position of postmaster.

As we might expect from the haphazard way in which their storekeeping was conducted, Berry and Lincoln at last completely failed. So they were quite willing to sell out to two brothers who offered to buy in the spring of 1833. These men gave their notes to Lincoln and his partner in payment, just as Berry and Lincoln had given theirs in the first place. It was an unfortunate transaction, for not long afterward both men disappeared without having paid anything. About the same time Lincoln's partner died, thus leaving all the debts for Lincoln to pay. They amounted to eight hundred dollars.

As we know, Lincoln was a poor man, and the only

work he could get was manual labor, which paid him very
little. But he went to the creditors and told them that he
would save up all the money that he could beyond what
he needed for his current expenses, and that in the end he
would pay them every dollar of the debt. It seemed to
him almost impossible that he should ever be clear of this
obligation. He used to speak of it as the national debt.
But he continued paying, even though it took him seventeen or eighteen years to pay the eleven hundred dollars
to which the debts with accrued interest amounted. He
had failed in business, but he had not failed in a high sense
of honor.

An incident which further reveals the firm honesty so
deeply ingrained in Lincoln's nature, belongs to this trying period and relates to his duties as postmaster. In
the remote villages in those early days, agents from the
Post-Office Department did not come around very often
to examine the accounts and collect the money due. It
was therefore several years after the post-office at New
Salem had closed, and while Lincoln was living in Springfield, that an agent came one day and asked for the
money, a sum amounting to something like seventeen
dollars, which was still due from New Salem to the Post-
Office Department. Lincoln at once went to a small trunk
standing in the corner of the little room which he used as
an office, and took out the exact sum which the agent
demanded, tied up in a cotton handkerchief. He handed

it over with the remark: "I never use any man's money but my own."

After his store "winked out," to use his own words, he had nothing to do but attend to the little post-office and take the odd jobs which came to his hand. Sometimes he went into the field and worked as a farm-hand. Sometimes he helped to straighten out the books in the store of his friend Ellis. It is very likely that he worked for his board oftener than for anything else. But, as we have seen in other cases, he was always a welcome guest in any farm-house. Every hard-working woman in the community would gladly put on an extra plate when Abraham Lincoln came to the house, or do extra darning or sewing for him whenever he needed help of that kind.

In the summer of 1833 a piece of good fortune came to him. John Calhoun, the county surveyor of Sangamon County, had more work than he could do, for the county was a large one and settlers were coming there in great numbers. Of course every landowner wished to have his farm surveyed and its boundaries marked out. Besides, in almost every county there was a group of men who wished to make money by speculating in land, upon which they hoped to locate towns or cities. All of this called for much work on the part of the surveyor.

So Calhoun, looking about for some man accurate and intelligent enough to help him, offered to appoint Lincoln as assistant county surveyor. In this position he would be able to earn three dollars a day. Here indeed was a bright opening, and Lincoln determined to study surveying and accept the offer.

He Studied Surveying Just as Thoroughly as He Had Studied Grammar

Getting a book on surveying, Lincoln again went out to his old friend Mentor Graham for help. With wonderful concentration the young man studied day and night— sometimes the whole night—for six weeks. By that time he had learned the subject so well that he could go out and survey a field accurately. But he had worked so hard that his health was in danger, and he became so haggard that his friends were greatly disturbed. He studied surveying just as thoroughly as he had studied grammar, and just as eagerly as he had read the Statutes of Indiana, or the dictionary in the earlier days of his youth.

This burning desire to know things clearly and thoroughly was a marked trait in him. We are told that during his boyhood it vexed him when he heard some one use a word which he could not understand. Quoting his own language, we have the following: "I can say this: that among my earliest recollections I remember how, when a mere child, I used to get irritated when any one talked to me in a way that I could not understand. I do not think that I got angry at anything else in my life. But that always disturbed my temper, and has ever since. I can remember going to my little bedroom after hearing the neighbors talk of an evening with my father, and spending no small part of the night walking up and down and trying to make out what was the exact meaning of some of their, to me, dark sayings.

"I could not sleep, although I tried to, when I got on such a hunt for an idea, until I had caught it; and when I thought I had got it, I was not satisfied until I had repeated it over and over; until I had put it in language plain enough, as I thought, for any boy I knew to comprehend. This was a kind of passion with me, and it always stuck by me; for I am never easy now, when I am handling a thought, till I have bounded it north and bounded it south, and bounded it east and bounded it west."

He was a good surveyor because he was careful and accurate. He was also called on often to settle boundary disputes, because of his fairness. This new occupation served also to extend his acquaintance. He met many people who became his warm and loyal friends and were of much value to him later in his public life.

One of them proved his friendship in a very practical way. In 1834 Lincoln was in a hard place. A man who held one of the notes which Berry and Lincoln gave when buying the stores in New Salem obtained judgment against him, and his horse, saddle, and surveying instruments were all sold in payment of the debt. This was a severe blow to the struggling young surveyor, for these were the means by which, according to his own words, he "procured bread and kept body and soul together." But his friend came to the rescue by purchasing Lincoln's property and then turning it over to him. Of course, when he could, Lincoln paid back to his friend all the money he had expended.

In 1834 Lincoln was again a candidate for the legislature, and this time he won the election. In the fall of that year he went to Vandalia, then the State capital, for his first

term. He did not make a brilliant record, but was observed to be a quiet, thoughtful young man, with good common sense and good nature. He was really at his university, learning, observing, thinking.

State-House at Vandalia where Lincoln Served as a Legislator in 1834-5

In 1835, after his first session, he returned to New Salem with a larger outlook on life. During the winter he had met some of the leading men of the State. He had had an opportunity to study them, to find out in what ways he was equal to them and in what ways he fell short, and he observed in all modesty that in many respects he was quite their equal.

His return to New Salem at this time was particularly happy for him, for there he had formed the acquaintance of a charming young woman, Ann Rutledge, who had completely won his affection and whom he now hoped to marry. In the latter part of 1832 he had gone to board at the Rutledge Tavern, kept by her father, and there he saw her every day.

She was beautiful and gentle, attractive in manner and strong in character. Such a young woman, of course, had many friends and also suitors, and she had become engaged to John McNeil, a young man who had come from New York to New Salem some years before. Although nothing was known about his family, he was regarded as a successful business man, for he had acquired enough money to buy a large farm not far from New Salem and also a half-interest in a general store in the village. It had been a case of love at first sight between him and Ann Rutledge. But in course of time McNeil became restless, and determined to return East. He told Ann that he would come back, bringing his father and mother, and then they would be married.

It was in the spring of 1834 that McNeil left for New York. As you know, travel by horse and afoot was slow in those days. Moreover, on the way across the continent McNeil fell ill with chills and fever. Ann Rutledge therefore had to wait a long time before she received any letter from her lover. Finally, after his arrival in New York late in the summer, he wrote; but then no further letters came. Lincoln, being postmaster, could not help knowing about any letters which Ann might receive or send. In fact, she seems to have made him her confidant in her anxiety.

Lincoln had long loved Ann; but he did not venture to reveal to her his affection until many months after McNeil had left, and his letters ceased to come. Then he told her of his love and begged her to become his wife. After a long time she consented, but Lincoln was so poor that it was necessary to wait until his prospects of a livelihood were better.

Now, on his return from the legislature he believed that he could at no distant day earn enough to make it safe for him to marry; and Ann promised to become his wife after she should have spent another year in school, and he meantime should be admitted to the bar.

The future looked happy to them both, and their friends in the village rejoiced with them. But after a few months Ann Rutledge became disturbed by torturing doubts. She wondered whether she was wronging her first lover; she wondered whether she was true to him; whether he would ever return; whether he still loved her, even though she loved another. These thoughts so wore upon her that she became seriously ill with a fever. Lincoln at first was not allowed to visit her, but she begged so earnestly to see him that at last he was permitted to go to her. It was the last time the two lovers ever saw each other, for shortly afterward Ann Rutledge died.

Lincoln was almost distracted with grief.   As his mother had been, he was subject to fits of melancholy, and the loss of that rare companionship was almost more than his sensitive soul could bear.   Heart and mind were rent, and for a time it was feared he might lose his reason.   He would walk for hours slowly along the river bank and through the forests, muttering strangely to himself, and his friends, believing he was on the verge of madness, kept a close watch on him for fear he might kill himself.

Ann Rutledge's body was buried in Concord Cemetery, about seven miles from New Salem.   There Lincoln frequently went to mourn over her grave.   After a time one of his most devoted friends, Bolin Green, took him to his own house, where he and his wife tenderly cared for him until he again became master of himself.   In the later years of his troubled life Lincoln never ceased to think of Ann Rutledge with tender memories.   He said: "I really and truly loved the girl and think often of her now."   Then, after a little pause, he added: ". . . and I have loved the name of Rutledge to this day."

But Abraham Lincoln was not the kind of man to give up to a sorrow even as heart-breaking as this.   In a short time he again took up active duties in preparation for the great life-work which lay before him.

CHAPTER IV

LAWYER AND CITIZEN IN SPRINGFIELD

In 1836 Lincoln was elected for his second term in the legislature. When this term closed (1837), he went back to New Salem. where he had lived for nearly six years. But he did not stay long, for he had determined to take up the practice of law in Springfield. Major Stuart, his adviser and friend, had invited him to come into his office as partner. This was an excellent opening for Lincoln, for Major Stuart held a leading place among the lawyers and politicians of the State and could therefore be helpful to him in securing business.

Lincoln had already been twice associated with Stuart in ways that brought them closely into touch with each other. For while Lincoln was captain of the company of volunteers in the Black Hawk War, Stuart was major in the same regiment; and both men had been elected as Whigs in 1834 to represent Sangamon County in the State legislature. It was during that campaign that Stuart advised Lincoln to become a lawyer; and after the election Lincoln took up the study of law seriously, although he had read law more or less before this time.

In the autumn of 1836 he received his license to practise law. and in April of the following year he was ready to

Lincoln in 1858—Age 49.

*From a photograph loaned by W. J. Franklin, of Macomb, Ill.,
after an ambrotype.*

Lincoln in 1858—Age 49.

From a photograph loaned by W. J. Franklin, of Macomb, Ill., after an ambrotype.

go to Springfield, which had now become, largely through his own influence in the legislature, the capital of the State. So he packed his scanty clothing and few effects into his saddle-bags and, borrowing a horse, left the place where life had held for him so much more of sorrow than of joy.

It was with some doubt as to the wisdom of his act that he gave up surveying, for he was making a fairly good living in that work, while success in the practice of law was as yet uncertain. His money obligations too were heavy. Very little of his store debt had been paid, and his father's family needed far more assistance from him than he could afford to give.

On arriving in Springfield he was much cast down. He was in one of his moods of deep depression and melancholy. He went directly to the store of his friend Joshua Speed, a prosperous young merchant, who tells in his own words the story of what happened, as follows:

"Lincoln had ridden into town on a borrowed horse, with no earthly property save a pair of saddle-bags containing a few clothes. I was a merchant at Springfield, and kept a large country store, embracing dry-goods, groceries, hardware, books, medicines, bedclothes, mattresses —in fact, everything that the country needed.

"Lincoln came into the store with his saddle-bags on his arm. He said he wanted to buy the furniture for a single bed. The mattress, blankets, sheets, coverlet, and pillow, according to the figures made by me, would cost seventeen dollars. He said that perhaps was cheap enough; but, small as the price was, he was unable to pay it. But if I would credit him till Christmas, and his experiment as a lawyer was a success, he would pay then; saying in the saddest tone, 'If I fail in this, I do not know that I can ever pay you.' As I looked up at him, I thought then, and I think now, that I never saw a sadder face.

"I said to him: 'You seem to be much pained at contracting so small a debt. I think I can suggest a plan by which you can avoid the debt and at the same time attain your end. I have a large room with a double bed upstairs, which you are welcome to share with me.'

"'Where is your room?' said he.

"'Up-stairs,' said I, pointing to a pair of winding stairs, which led from the store to my room.

"He took his saddle-bags on his arm, went up-stairs, set them on the floor, and came down, with the most changed expression of countenance. Beaming with pleasure, he exclaimed: 'Well, Speed, I am moved.'"

Lincoln was fortunate in being associated as partner with a man so prominent as Major Stuart, for this partnership of itself helped to give him a good standing in the community. From the first he was willing to do his part as a citizen of Springfield, and took an interest in all phases of the community life. Here, too, as in New Salem, he easily made friends of all because he was helpful and took a kindly interest in the life of those about him. He recognized everybody he met on the street, and he seemed to have time to talk with any friend or neighbor who was in a talkative mood. Moreover, he took an interest in everything going on, in every house that was built, in every street that was opened. He joined a group of young men in forming a debating club, and in other ways he played his part in the intellectual life of the town, which then contained about fifteen hundred people. He was also more or less identified with the social life about him, although this was not the kind of life that appealed to him most.

Within two years from the time when he went to Springfield to live he met a young woman belonging to a prominent Kentucky family. This was Miss Mary Todd. She was now making her home with her sister, who was the wife of Ninian Edwards, one of Lincoln's political friends. The Edwards family was one of influence in Springfield.

Miss Todd, who was proud-spirited and ambitious for social position, took a leading part in the social life of the town. Brought up among the refinements of life, and being brilliant, witty, and well-educated, she received attention from many young men. It was soon evident, however, that Mr. Lincoln held the first place in her esteem.

The friendship between Lincoln and Miss Todd grew rapidly, but Mr. and Mrs. Edwards opposed her accepting Lincoln as a suitor. They said he had been brought up in a poor and humble home; that he was careless about social forms and indifferent to social life. But the young woman knew her own mind. She seemed to believe, after a brief acquaintance with the awkward young lawyer, that he would in time fill positions of large influence in his State and country. She even predicted that he would become President of the United States. Sometime in 1840 Abraham Lincoln and Miss Todd became engaged to be married.

It was not long before there was more or less disagreement between the two lovers, so different were they in experience, tastes, and ambitions in life. Lincoln's world was not that of society; and therefore in certain little ways that count in social life he was lacking. He often failed, for instance, to go with Miss Todd to social gatherings, thereby causing misunderstandings, which sometimes led to quarrels between the two; and it did not take long for Lincoln to learn that love-making with this brilliant, proud young woman was not all sunshine. There were many stormy experiences, and he began to doubt whether he could ever make her happy. As time went on, his doubts increased, and he made up his mind that he and Miss Todd were not suited to each other. After long and painful hesitation, therefore, he broke the engagement.

Then followed a period of gloom and despair like that which came after the death of Ann Rutledge. It was plain to Lincoln that the young woman loved him and, always deeply sensitive in matters of conscience, he feared that he had done her an injustice. So harrowing became his sorrow and distress that all the melancholy in his temperament asserted itself, and he declared he could never be happy again.

During the summer of 1842, however, through the good offices of friends the lovers were brought together again, and their former relations were restored. One morning the two young people suddenly informed Mrs. Edwards that they had decided to be married without delay.

The Edwards Residence, Springfield, where Lincoln Was Married.

The whole affair was so unexpected that no elaborate ceremony was possible, and the bride even found it necessary to borrow a wedding-gown from a sister who had been recently married. The wedding took place in the autumn of 1842, and the young couple at once began life in a simple way, in a modest hotel, where they paid four dollars a week for their board.

Meanwhile Lincoln was going on with the practice of law, and at the same time he was helping to make new laws, for he was elected to the State legislature for four successive terms, serving continuously for eight years— from 1834 to 1842.

As a legislator he was active, and became so prominent that the Whigs nominated him for speaker, but they, being in the minority, could not elect their candidate. While it is true that he was a leader in his party, it must be admitted that such economic and political questions as were before the people at that time did not make a strong appeal to his nature. It was the great moral questions like human slavery that were of absorbing interest to him and that called into action all that was best in him, as we are to see later.

Where Stuart and Lincoln Had Their Law-Office
in 1837.

Still his legislative experience was of much value in preparing him for the great work of his later career, and it brought to public notice, in an emphatic way, his moral courage on the slavery question. For he had the distinction of leading a minority of two, in a written declaration that they, he and one other, believed the institution of slavery was founded on both injustice and bad policy. Having a strong conviction that slavery was an evil, he was quite willing to face overwhelming opposition to his views, no matter what might be the effect upon his own political fortunes.

In 1846 he was elected to represent Illinois in the national Congress at Washington. Here he was the same plain, simple man that he had always been, modest in dress, homely in speech, and sincere in manner. It was his habit when getting books at the library to tie them up in a bandanna handkerchief. Then, slipping his cane through a knot of the handkerchief, he would sling the books over his shoulder and, quite unmindful of the smiles of those he met, he quietly went his way, deeply absorbed in his own thoughts.

His first story in the lounging-room of the House attracted the attention of all who heard it, and in a short time he came to be known as the champion story-teller in Congress. It is doubtful, in fact, whether Lincoln ever met his match in quaint, droll humor and in his ability to tell effective jokes, stories, and anecdotes. By these he won the favor of Daniel Webster to such an extent as to be more than once a guest at the Saturday morning breakfasts given by the great orator from Massachusetts.

Abraham Lincoln had not been in Congress many weeks before he introduced what are known as his "spot" resolutions, which became a stumbling-block for his re-election.

In so doing he tried to show, as a Whig, that the Democratic administration—James K. Polk was President—was wrong in declaring that the Mexicans brought on the war with Mexico by attacking American troops on American

Lincoln Telling Stories in the Lounging-Room of Congress.

soil. The "spot" where the first blood was shed, according to Lincoln, was not American soil but disputed territory, which was claimed by Mexico. Lincoln insisted that the United States Government was unjust in going into this war. But, though he stoutly held to this position as a matter of principle, yet he always voted with the ma-

jority when it was a question of granting supplies to the army fighting our battles on Mexican territory.

He believed that the war had been brought about for the purpose of increasing slave territory in the United States, and this he bitterly opposed. So, when David Wilmot introduced a bill into Congress excluding slavery from all territory which the United States might acquire as a result of the war, Lincoln strongly favored it. He said afterward that he voted for the Wilmot Proviso some forty times.

Before his term of office as Congressman came to an end he introduced a bill to abolish slavery in the District of Columbia. According to this bill, slavery "was to be ended in the national capital with the consent of the voters and with compensation to slave-owners." Although this bill failed, because it was in advance of public opinion, it showed Lincoln's firm resolution to do all he could to restrict the institution of slavery in this country.

CHAPTER V

LIFE AS A LAWYER ON THE CIRCUIT

AT the close of Lincoln's term in Congress (1849) he determined to retire from politics and take up again the practice of law.

This was for two reasons. The first was that the position he had taken in regard to the Mexican War had made him so unpopular that he knew he could not carry the next election from his State, even if he should wish to do so. His term in Congress had added nothing to the political favor in which he was held. Again overtaken by depression, he even questioned his fitness for political life, and it seemed to him more than likely that he would never go into politics again. The second reason was that his financial outlook was by no means promising. The debt from his storekeeping experience at New Salem still hung heavy about his neck, and his own growing family, although he lived very simply, was becoming more expensive. In addition to these burdens, his father's family still looked to him for some of the necessaries and about all of the comforts of life. Whether he had to furnish money to prevent the foreclosure of a mortgage on his father's farm, or to pay doctors' bills, or to meet other expense, his father's family was always more or less of a drain upon his purse.

73

We must bear in mind, also, that Lincoln was not by nature a money-maker. His income from his law practice was never large, not more than three thousand dollars a year. It might easily have been more, but his fees were small, and oftentimes he charged nothing for his services, especially when he thought the client too poor to pay. Naturally, his brother lawyers objected to this generous habit, on the ground that Lincoln thus lowered the standard of charges for legal services; but his love of fair play was stronger than his sense of money values.

His plainly furnished law-office was in keeping with his character. It contained a chair, a lounge, and a desk— not that he needed the desk to write upon, for more frequently it served as a foot-rest, while he supported on his knees the book on which he wrote. Surroundings did not affect him. He could withdraw his mind from any confusion about him, and had no difficulty in marshalling the facts of his well-ordered knowledge just when he wanted to use them. He kept his notes and memoranda on slips of paper, which he stowed away in his hat, a habit formed in the earlier days when he was postmaster at New Salem.

Although Lincoln's office was in Springfield, his business took him over a wide stretch of country, for in those days it was not possible in the West for lawyers to make a good living in any one place. Their practice extended over what was known as a circuit; that is, one of several divisions in a State set apart under an appointed judge, who travelled from county-seat to county-seat. The judge made the circuit twice a year, and with him travelled some of the best-known lawyers of the district. Lincoln's circuit was the "Eighth Judicial Circuit." It was one hundred and fifty miles long, one hundred and fifty miles broad, and contained from twelve to fifteen counties.

This kind of law practice strongly appealed to Lincoln, for he liked travelling from county to county in company with the circuit judge and the other lawyers to attend courts when they were in session. Alert-minded and always open to new impressions, he felt an interest in the people he met, and in everything he saw on the highways, in the fields, and on the farms. And while sometimes he would sit silent and absorbed, with a sad, brooding expression, most of the time he was the life and joy of the company, seeing humor and entertainment in all the small, homely incidents on the way. It might be men working in the field, ducks waddling to a pond, a washing flapping in the wind, almost anything that would catch his fancy, and keep the crowd in a continuous rollicking mood to their journey's end.

An incident of this period, told by a brother lawyer, reveals his care and tenderness for helpless creatures. He had been riding one day with a group of fellow lawyers when he was missed by his companions. One of them, going back to look for him, found that he had stopped to replace two young birds that had been blown out of their

nest. "I couldn't have slept," he said, "if I had not restored them to their mother."

As there were no railroads in Illinois until 1850, travel
was generally on horseback; but sometimes several lawyers
would join in getting a three-seated spring wagon. At
first Lincoln rode on a borrowed horse, but later he bought
one for himself, which he called "Old Tom." After his return from Washington, he added to his turnout an old open
buggy. The pokey horse, the rattletrap buggy, and Lincoln made one of the most interesting pictures of the days
of circuit-riding.

His dress was often wrinkled and rusty. Sometimes
he wore a low-crowned hat and sometimes a shaggy beaver.
For a long time his coat was a short blue one, which reached
only to his hips. He usually carried a little old hand-bag,
and a faded, weather-beaten umbrella tied with a string
to keep it from flapping.

Of course, Lincoln did not appear so peculiar amid the
pioneer conditions surrounding him as he would have
done in a part of the country which had long been settled.
The dress of the people living in such a backwoods region
as Illinois, at that time, was distinctly different from what
could be found in a long-settled State, Massachusetts, for
instance, or Virginia. But it must be said that at best
Lincoln was always indifferent to dress and careless about
clothes.

There were few roads such as we know to-day, and no

bridges at all. The streams had to be forded, and as Lincoln was tall he sometimes rolled up his trousers and tested the depth of the water by wading across to the other side. Then the others would follow.

Whenever They Stopped for Dinner Lincoln Was the Life of the Company.

Whenever in their journeyings they stopped for dinner at a farmhouse, Lincoln again was the life of the company. Everybody along the circuit liked him, because of his kindness and good cheer.

The comfort of travelling in those days was far removed from what it is to-day, and Lincoln's good nature

and drollery must have been very helpful in relieving unpleasant situations for his brother lawyers, who did not
hesitate to grumble at what they considered hardships.
The taverns at the county-seats were usually two-story
houses, with large rooms and long verandas. The judge
and the lawyers slept two in a bed, with three or four beds
in a room. There was a common table where judge, jury,
lawyers, prisoners, peddlers, and all ate together, the upper
end of the table being reserved for the judge and his lawyers.
But Lincoln was as likely to sit at one end as the other.
At the tavern he met with a hearty welcome from all, for
he was the best-known and the best-loved lawyer on the
circuit. At every county-seat were a few houses of pre-
tension, where formal entertainments were given during
the court session. At these functions Lincoln was always
an appreciated guest.

But the place most to his liking was the court-house.
This was generally a small square building of red brick,
trimmed with white and surmounted by a cupola. In the
one room it contained the judge held his court, the lawyers
pleaded their cases, and the jury listened and deliberated.
The cases were mostly simple ones concerning boundaries,
deeds, trespasses, etc. The lawyers and their clients consulted in little groups apart, under the trees, or at the side
of the building, or wherever they could find a quiet corner.

Lincoln's advice was always to settle, if possible, without a trial. Lawyers, he thought, should work for peace;

even then there would be plenty of cases for all. So we may imagine him laboring first with his client, before he turns the force of his clear, plain arguments upon the listening judge and jury. Here is what he says to a young man who complains about his guardian: "I know Mr. Kingsbury, and he is not the man to have cheated you out of a cent, and I can't take the case, and I advise you to drop it."

Lincoln was an especial favorite with Judge David Davis, a man of force and much learning, who for many years presided over the courts in the Eighth Circuit while Lincoln practised there. Unless he was present in the company which gathered in the judge's room after supper, his Honor seemed to be dissatisfied. He would constantly interrupt the conversation with such impatient questions as "Where's Lincoln? Why doesn't Lincoln come?" And when the genial, good-natured Lincoln did appear and begin to tell the stories which delighted all the listeners, the judge rebuked any man who dared to interrupt, with the stern remark: "Mr. Lincoln is talking."

Although while out of court the judge was somewhat indifferent to formality, he was very insistent when in the court-room upon good order and serious attention to the work in hand. When Lincoln was not busy he was often whispering stories to his neighbors. This sometimes annoyed Judge Davis, who would then call him to order.

"I was never fined but once for contempt of court."

said a clerk at one of the county-seats in Lincoln's day. "Judge Davis fined me five dollars. Mr. Lincoln had just come in, and leaning over my desk, he told me a story so irresistibly funny that I broke out into a loud laugh. The judge called me to order in haste, saying: 'This must be stopped. Mr. Lincoln, you are constantly disturbing this court with your stories.' Then to me: 'You may fine yourself five dollars for your disturbance.' I apologized, but told the judge that the story was worth the money. In a few minutes the judge called me to him. 'What was the story Lincoln told you?' he asked. I told him and he laughed aloud in spite of himself. 'Remit your fine,' he ordered."

As a lawyer Lincoln had great power over a jury, but this was not through any attempt at oratory. His method was to get at the heart of the matter, to present it plainly and simply so that it could be clearly understood. He had a good knowledge of law, but it was his instinct for right and justice that enabled him to strip away unnecessary detail, and present his case in a practical way to the jury. For this purpose he made free use of stories—not to amuse his juries, as some have supposed, but to make them see the case clearly and to avoid long arguments. One of the lawyers who knew him said: "In making a speech Mr. Lincoln was the plainest man I ever heard. He was not a speaker but a talker. He talked to jurors and to political gatherings plain, sensible, candid talk, almost as in conversation, making no effort whatever at oratory. But his talk had wonderful effect. Honesty, candor, fairness, everything that was convincing, was in his manner and expression."

Lincoln could not take the side which he believed was wrong. In order to convince others, he must himself believe that his cause was right and just. It was simply impossible for him to argue against his convictions. To do so he believed would be dishonest, and he could no more be dishonest in this way than he could steal. It happened once that, during the course of a case he was trying, he became sure of his client's guilt. Suddenly he turned to his associate and whispered: "Swift, the man is guilty. You defend him; I cannot." And immediately he gave up his share of the fee, which was large enough to mean a great deal to him. At another time, while he was defending a man on trial, he turned to his associate with the remark: "If you can say anything for the man, do it. I cannot. If I attempt it, the jury will see I think he is guilty and convict him." He then gave up the case.

The informal ways of the court and the familiar footing of Lincoln with his juries is well illustrated by the Armstrong case. In the course of his law practice he was sent for by Jack Armstrong's widow, who asked him to defend her son, who was charged with murder. You will remember the Jack Armstrong with whom he had the wrestling-match at New Salem and who had become his lifelong friend.

When Jack Armstrong's widow asked him to take the case, he cheerfully complied, insisting that he would charge nothing for his services.

The principal witness against young Armstrong declared that he saw the prisoner strike the blow which caused the death of the murdered man. Lincoln asked: "When did

you see the blow struck?"

The witness answered: "It was about ten o'clock at night."

"How could you see plainly at that hour?" asked Lincoln.

"Why," was the answer, "the moon was full

Court-House at Beardstown, in Which the Armstrong Case Was Tried.

and was shining so brightly that it was as high as the sun is about ten o'clock in the morning."

Lincoln then turned to an almanac and showed that at ten o'clock on the night named the moon was in its last quarter, and was almost setting. This unexpected turn in the case of course set at naught the value of the witness's testimony, and produced a great effect upon the feeling of the jury and the people in the court-room.

In addressing the jury Lincoln said that it was a pleasure to him to give his services to help clear from a false charge the son of his old friend. He then told of the days when, homeless and almost friendless, he used to go to the log cabin of the Armstrongs, where he found food and shelter, and where his worn clothing was mended by the kindly mother of the prisoner. Lincoln made such a pathetic appeal that the tears rolled down the cheeks of the jurors, some of whom had known him in those days; and every man, when the jury filed back into the court-room, returned a verdict of "Not Guilty."

Lincoln's law cases were not limited to those in the circuit courts. He argued many, and some were very important ones, in the supreme court of Illinois, showing that he was one of the leading lawyers of the State. In one of these cases Lincoln was counsel for the Illinois Central Railroad—a railroad of which George B. McClellan later became vice-president. His high standing was recognized by his being engaged as associate counsel in a famous patent case in 1855 in Cincinnati. His client, the manufacturer of the McCormick reaper, had four hundred thousand dollars at stake.

When, however, he found that the opposing counsel was an eminent lawyer from the East, he lost confidence in Lincoln, the country lawyer, whom he had engaged on another's recommendation, and called in Edwin M. Stanton, of Ohio, to assist. Stanton paid little attention to the awkward, raw-boned man from the backwoods, as he appeared to him, and evidently looked upon Lincoln as inferior. He was heard to say in a scornful tone: "Where did that long-armed creature come from, and what can he expect from this case?" So, almost ignoring Lincoln, Stanton took upon himself the burden of making the speech to the jury, and thus without Lincoln's assistance won the case. This was a keen disappointment to Lincoln and his friends, for they had hoped that he would have an opportunity to win distinction. But there came a time, as we shall learn later, when this same Edwin M. Stanton learned to respect and admire the true Lincoln and to follow his leadership.

Lincoln's term in Congress, although it interrupted his law practice, proved a great benefit, for it inspired him with a renewed zest to increase his knowledge. His experiences in Washington had given the opportunity to study the leaders in Congress, and he keenly realized that the training of these men was very much better than his own. In their public speaking they had shown a power of close and sustained reasoning which he could not command but was ambitious to acquire. So when he gave up political life and returned to the practice of law, he had resolved to apply himself to make good, if possible, the deficiency of his early training, and thus be able to meet these well-trained lawyers on equal terms. Books and study once more became a passion with him.

Lincoln in 1860.

*From an ambrotype taken in Springfield, Ill., in the collection of William
H. Lambert, of Philadelphia.*

Mathematics, astronomy, and poetry were the subjects he now took up. He even joined a class of young men who were learning German, inviting them to meet in his office. With the same care and thoroughness that he had devoted to English grammar years before, he now studied geometry, learning six books of Euclid by heart.

This close application to books made it impossible to spend so much time with his brother lawyers as he formerly had done. Now, after he had told a story, he would often slip away while the listeners were laughing at the climax. At night, when "riding the circuit," it became his habit to read, sometimes until two o'clock in the morning, by the light of a candle standing on a chair near the head of his bed. But notwithstanding the late hour when he went to sleep, he was usually up before any of the others, and when they opened their eyes they would see him sitting before the fire with the coals uncovered, musing and pondering.

A very agreeable and charming side of Lincoln's personality is seen in his home life during this period. While careless of conventions, he was by no means negligent of the virtues for which they stood. As a home-maker he bore his part in the responsibilities of the family life, and was especially delightful as a host. It was a pleasure among the Lincolns' friends to be bidden to their home, for Mrs. Lincoln was an efficient hostess, always providing an abundant table with delicious Southern cooking, and was tactful in putting her guests at ease, while Mr. Lincoln with his cordial welcome afforded rich entertainment by his store of anecdotes and his unrivalled conversation.

As a father he was most affectionate and lenient. His three boys—Robert, born in 1843, Willie in 1849, and Tad (Thomas) in 1853—regarded their father as their best play-fellow. He rarely went down-town from his home in Springfield without the two younger boys, carrying one perhaps on his back, while the other clung to his hand.

On one occasion a neighbor was called to his door by the cries of two boys. Looking out, he saw Mr. Lincoln striding by with a boy on either side of him, each one crying at the top of his voice.

"Why, Mr. Lincoln, what's the matter with the boys?" his neighbor asked.

"Just what's the matter with the whole world," he answered. "I've got three walnuts and each wants two."

His sense of humor was always keen, and stood out in striking contrast with the melancholy which often dom-inated his thoughts and feelings for hours or even days at a time.

Thus we see that up to 1854, Lincoln lived a simple, natural, industrious life, not unlike that of many another ambitious young man born in a log cabin on the Western frontier. Yet, in the light of later events, it is clear that unconsciously he was preparing for the large responsibilities awaiting him, and that always under the surface of his life an eternal purpose seemed to be working its way.

The qualities of heart which were his in so generous measure—honesty, charity, and sympathy for the suffering—were the qualities peculiarly needed for the great mission to which he was called. Through his experience as a lawyer, also, he was gaining a knowledge of men, and was developing the habits of clear thinking and just reasoning which were soon to be applied to a great issue involving the nation. That issue we are now to take up.

CHAPTER VI

THE LINCOLN–DOUGLAS DEBATES

You will remember that when Lincoln returned to his home in Springfield after his term in Congress was over, he determined to give up politics and devote his entire energy to the study of law. At that time he believed that he would never enter the political field again, but only five years passed before a public event so aroused him that he changed his mind. This was the repeal of the Missouri Compromise in 1854. It took such a hold upon his feelings that he could scarcely talk about anything else.

We shall better understand why he was so disturbed over this repeal if we briefly review the slavery troubles that were straining the relations between the North and the South.

Before the purchase of the Louisiana territory,—which, as you know, meant nearly everything west of the Mississippi, from Arkansas to Canada and west to Utah and Idaho—all the States north of Mason and Dixon's line and the Ohio River were free States, while the other States, those south of that line, were slave States. This was not according to any law of the nation, but on account of the nature of the soil and climate. With the purchase of

Louisiana, however, many new States would, in time, be added to the Union, and the question of how many should be slave and how many should be free had to be settled, because the vast new profits from raising cotton had made the South eager to extend slave territory and the feeling against slavery was growing strong in the North. This question the Missouri Compromise was supposed to decide. It provided that Missouri should come into the Union as a slave State but that all the remaining territory in the Louisiana Purchase which lay west and north of Missouri should be forever free.

There was no further serious trouble over slavery in new States until the end of the Mexican War. Then, by the Compromise of 1850, it was provided that California should come into the Union as a free State, and that in all the rest of the territory acquired from Mexico—that is, in what were then the territories of Utah and New Mexico —the people should decide for themselves whether or not they would have slavery.

Of course, in a compromise—a sort of half-way meeting —neither side gets everything it wishes. Each has to give up something to the other. Yet, when the Compromise of 1850 was agreed upon, both Northern and Southern political leaders honestly believed that the slavery controversy was settled for all time. But it was not. In 1854, under the able leadership of Senator Stephen A. Douglas, of Illinois, another bill, the Kansas-Nebraska Bill, was passed. This provided that in the territory lying north and west of Missouri—that territory in the Louisiana Purchase which by the Missouri Compromise was made forever free—the people should decide for themselves whether or not they would have slavery. This bill thrust aside, or repealed, the Missouri Compromise and put in its place "the right of popular sovereignty," as Douglas called it.

This disregard of the Missouri Compromise aroused Lincoln as perhaps nothing had ever aroused him before. It was a great wrong, he believed,

Stephen A. Douglas.

and the thought haunted him day and night. It seemed to take complete possession of him. All his life he had believed that slavery was wrong, because he believed no man had a right to own another. Yet he had no idea of interfering with slavery in the States that already had it; for in all those States any man had just as firm a legal right, according to the Constitution of the United States, to own slaves as he had to own houses and land, or any other kind of property.

But Lincoln was strongly, even bitterly, opposed to the extension of slavery into new States. Moreover, quite apart from the human injustice and wrong of slavery, was the violation of his sense of the uprightness of law; for he regarded slavery compromises like the Missouri Compromise just as morally binding as the Constitution itself, and considered that, in thrusting it aside, the framers of the Kansas-Nebraska Bill were breaking the law of the nation. He therefore determined to use all the powers of his being to get the law restored, and to prevent Kansas from coming into the Union as a slave State.

So it was the Kansas-Nebraska Bill, repealing the Missouri Compromise, that called Abraham Lincoln back into politics and summoned him to take up his great life mission, which involved a resolute and unwavering opposition to the extension of slavery. It was as if a higher power said to him: "This is your work. Do it, no matter what may be the cost to you in time, strength, or political advancement."

Opposition to the extension of slavery was the one fundamental issue upon which the Republican party was built. Lincoln was so strongly in sympathy with this doctrine that, although up to this time he had been a Whig, he joined the Republican party when in 1856 it was organized in the State of Illinois, at a convention held in Bloomington.

After this convention had adopted a platform, elected delegates to the Republican National Convention, and nominated State officers, it called upon certain men present for speeches. None of them seemed to make much impression. But finally the audience shouted, "Lincoln! Lincoln!" again and again. Slowly his tall form rose in the back part of the room, and moved forward to the platform. His countenance seemed to be burdened by a great weight. It was plain that he thought of this as a crisis in his life, a great opportunity. It was the moment when he was about to announce himself as no longer a Whig but from that time on a Republican.

As he turned to look at his eager listeners his face changed, a great passion laid hold upon him, and he seemed to grow in stature. At first he talked slowly, even haltingly; but in a little while, when deep emotion swayed him, he spoke with greater force. His eyes blazed with excitement, his face became pale, and his voice was vibrant with deep feeling. As he grew more and more intense his auditors started from their seats with white faces and quivering lips, moving toward the speaker. Men and women cheered and cried at the same time. In a little while all present seemed to feel and think and will as one man, and Lincoln had made them Republicans not only in name but also in spirit.

"The conclusion of all is," said Lincoln, in his closing words, "that we must restore the Missouri Compromise. We must highly resolve that Kansas must be free!"

"The greatest speech ever made in Illinois, and it puts Lincoln on the track for the presidency," was the comment made by many enthusiastic Republicans present.

Many newspaper men who came to make reports of the speeches were held so spellbound that they put their pens and pencils aside. "I attended for about fifteen minutes," says Mr. Herndon, Lincoln's law partner, "as it was usual with me then to make notes, but at the end of that time I threw pen and paper away and lived only in the inspiration of the hour."

It required courage for Abraham Lincoln to make this speech, for in doing so he was not only defending an unpopular cause, but he was giving up his place in an old and well-grounded political party to join a new and unpopular one. Yet it set him apart as the right man for leadership of the Republican party in Illinois, for it gave unmistakable evidence of his fearless spirit and of his stubborn resolve to fight to the bitter end in the cause of righteousness, justice, and humanity. He believed in his cause, and he believed in God; so he took up the fight.

Men soon began to follow him with admiration and enthusiasm. Day by day, slowly but steadily, he won others to his way of thinking until, two years after his eloquent speech before the Bloomington convention, he had become so influential in his party that his nomination for the United States Senate in the approaching Republican convention of the State of Illinois seemed to be a certainty. As the day drew near for this convention to meet (June 16, 1858), Lincoln was observed from time to time to make notes on such scraps of papers and old envelopes as happened to be convenient, and to put them in the crown of his hat. He sought no one's advice, nor confided in any one, until the day before the convention; when, having his speech well thought out, he took it to a number of his friends. The part of it which was likely to receive most criticism was as follows:

"A house divided against itself cannot stand. I believe this government cannot endure permanently half slave and half free. I do not expect the Union to be dissolved—I do not expect the house to fall—but I do expect it will cease to be divided. It will become all one thing or all the other. Either the opponents of slavery will arrest the further spread of it, and place it where the public mind can rest in the belief that it is in the course of ultimate extinction; or its advocates will push it forward until it shall become alike lawful in all States, old as well as new, North as well as South."

When he read these words to his friends, only one of them, Herndon his partner, approved. Herndon said: "Lincoln, deliver that speech as read and it will make you President." All the others strongly denounced it as unwise, foolish, and inviting disaster. But Lincoln said: "Friends, this thing has been retarded long enough. The time has come when these sentiments should be uttered; and if it is decreed that I should go down because of this speech, then let me go down linked with the truth. Let me die in the advocacy of what is just and right."

The next day he made the speech without the change of a single word, and to one critic he said later: "If I had to draw a pen across my record and erase my whole life from sight, but had one poor gift or choice left as to what I should save from the wreck, I should choose that speech and leave it to the world unerased."

Douglas in his public speeches made a strong point of the house-divided-against-itself part of Lincoln's speech. He said: "It is sectional, and it proves that Lincoln is an Abolitionist." This was giving a wrong impression, for Abolitionists believed in doing away with slavery in all the States, and that was quite a different matter from what Lincoln was trying to have done, which was to restrict it to the States in which it already existed.

Douglas kept criticising Lincoln's position without directly meeting his arguments, until at the end of a month Lincoln resolved to make him face the issue squarely. So he challenged the senator to a series of debates. Douglas accepted the challenge, and it was arranged to hold seven joint debates in various parts of the State.

The two debaters were very different in appearance and

training and, to the minds of most people, quite unequal, Douglas appearing to be much the superior of the two. Although he was then only forty-five years old, he was the most brilliant leader in the Democratic party. His rise in the political world had caught public attention. When only twenty-eight he had filled a place on the bench of the State supreme court. At thirty-one he had been a member of Congress, and for eleven years he had been in the United States Senate, where he held a place of national prominence. After the deaths of Henry Clay, Daniel Webster, and John C. Calhoun, he was the member most powerful in debate and had been at least a match for the three most distinguished senators—Charles Sumner, William H. Seward, and Salmon P. Chase. He was short in stature, hardly five feet four inches tall; but his broad shoulders, his massive and majestic head, and his deep and powerful voice helped to make him a most impressive speaker. Besides, he was not only well-dressed and prosperous-looking, but he appeared to be perfectly at home on the public platform, where his personal magnetism and unusual gifts of oratory gave him great power over his audience.

Lincoln's position in contrast was almost pathetic. To be sure, he had served eight years in the State legislature and one term in Congress, but at the end of this term his record had been accounted so nearly a failure that, as already noted, he had retired from public life. Even now, at the age of forty-nine, he was a country lawyer with no follow-

ing outside of his own State. His greatest source of strength
was the truth which he wished to present, and this of course
did not appear at the outset. So, as he rose before an
audience, they saw only a tall, gaunt figure towering six
feet four inches in height, clothed in garments that hung
loosely upon his ill-jointed frame. When he began to
speak, his shoulders drooped as if he were weak and uncertain of himself. His high tenor voice in moments of
excitement was shrill and piercing. But there was in his
sad face a sincerity, in his manner a modesty, and in his
words a simplicity, which spoke directly to the heart and
gave a convincing quality to his words. Moreover, when
swayed by deep emotion his voice became soft and musical,
and people listened to him with breathless interest.

Lincoln realized quite as completely as any one could
the striking contrast between himself and his powerful opponent. "With me," he said in melancholy tones, when
he was comparing his own career with that of Douglas,
"the race of ambition has been a failure—a flat failure.
With him it has been one of splendid success." But, notwithstanding this feeling, he entered upon the great contest with unflinching courage, with the assurance that,
however weak he might be in himself, his purpose was
upright and his cause was just.

Immense crowds swarmed to these meetings. Men,
women, and children came from long distances, in wagons,
in carriages, on horseback, and afoot. Many brought food,

Lincoln in 1860.
From a photograph by Hesler, copyright by George B. Ayres.

Lincoln in 1860.
From a photograph by Hesler, copyright by George B. Ayres.

and some brought bedding also. At night they encamped in the fields and groves surrounding the town where the meeting was held, till the camp-fires suggested the gathering of an army.

Before the second debate, Lincoln called some of his political friends together and asked their advice about some questions which he thought of putting to Douglas. One of these was as follows:

"Can the people of a United States Territory, in any lawful way, exclude slavery from its limits prior to the formation of a State constitution?"

This was a trying question, for if Douglas answered "No" the North would not like it; if he said "Yes" the South would be displeased.

Most of Lincoln's friends advised him not to ask the question. They said: "If you do, you will make a serious mistake. If Douglas says 'Yes' you will lose the senatorship."

Lincoln, with great confidence, responded: "I am after larger game; if Douglas answers this question in such a way as to win the senatorship, he will lose the presidency in 1860, and that battle is worth a hundred of this."

The next day Lincoln's friends noted that he mounted the platform with a firmer step and a more confident manner than he had done at the time of the first debate. Moreover, he asked the question just as he had presented it to them in the first place. Douglas's answer was: "The people of a Territory can, by unfriendly legislation, exclude slavery from a Territory before the formation of a State constitution." This answer reassured the North and helped Douglas to win the senatorship. But when the knowledge of it reached the people of the South, they were indignant. They declared that Douglas had betrayed them and that he had repudiated the Dred Scott Decision.

The Dred Scott Decision, as you should know, had been given out in 1857 by the Supreme Court. It declared that a negro was not a citizen, and that slave-owners had a right to take their slaves into a Territory and hold them there as slaves just as they had to hold them in a slave State. In other words, masters might take their slaves to any part of the Union just as they or anybody else might take cattle, horses, or any other kind of personal property.

Lincoln showed the contradictory nature of Douglas's position on the use of unfriendly legislation to shut slavery out of a Territory, where, by the Dred Scott Decision, it had a right to be, in the following words:

"The judge holds that a thing may be lawfully driven away from a place where it has a lawful right to be."

At the last of the debates Lincoln uttered, in closing, these impressive words: "Is slavery wrong? That is the real issue. That is the issue that will continue in this country when these poor tongues of Judge Douglas and myself shall be silent. It is the eternal struggle between these two principles—right and wrong—throughout the world."

While these debates were going on both Lincoln and Douglas had to endure considerable hardship in their long journeyings. But Douglas's movements were something like a triumphal procession. Much of the time he travelled in the luxurious private car of George B. McClellan, vice-president of the Illinois Central Railroad Company, for this company—the real terminus of the railroad being at New Orleans and much of its business coming from the South—was opposed to the Republican party. A brass band travelled with him, and attached to his car was a platform which carried a cannon. On the arrival of Douglas's train in a town where a debate was to be held, there was fired a salute of thirty-two guns, one for each of the thirty-two States. Then, riding in a handsome equipage, and escorted by his brass band, Douglas made his way to the tavern, his admirers greeting him with enthusiasm along the way. Much of the time Mrs. Douglas, a woman of fine presence and of gracious manner, accompanied her husband and exercised no small influence in his favor.

In striking contrast to this method of travel, Lincoln occupied a half-seat in an ordinary coach; or, if there was no coach, rode in a freight-car, although on some occasions he had to travel during the night. He had not an independent fortune like Douglas, but was a poor man and therefore had to be careful about the expenditure of money.

The only time when he travelled in state was when he went to some out-of-the-way place not on the railroad to

make a speech between debates. On such an occasion a
distinguished citizen would meet Lincoln at the station

Lincoln Greeted by Enthusiasts during the Lincoln-Douglas Debates.

nearest the town where he was to speak and take him in a
carriage. When within two or three miles of the town
they would be met by a procession of citizens with banners

and music. Then there was a speech of greeting and welcome, and the women on the entertainment committee
presented Lincoln with flowers, and sometimes, although
not to his liking, they hung a garland around his neck.

These seven joint debates extended over a period of
many weeks. It was very hard upon the debaters, for
almost every day of the time they spoke publicly at least
once. Each of them, in fact, made not less than one hundred speeches during this remarkable campaign. Douglas
spent lavishly, as he could afford to do, and the campaign
cost him something like eighty thousand dollars. Lincoln
had to spend carefully, but the expenses of his campaign
footed up to nearly a thousand dollars, an insignificant
sum compared with Douglas's, but yet much more than
he was able to pay. "I am absolutely without money,"
declared Lincoln at the time, "even for household expenses." You see it meant much for him that during all
these weeks he had not only had to make what was for
him a heavy outlay of money, but he had earned nothing,
or next to nothing, by his law practice.

The election for the Senate took place in early autumn.
Lincoln received a majority of five thousand on the popular
vote, but the legislature gave Douglas a majority of eight,
and therefore elected him to the United States Senate.

Although it was a victory for the "Little Giant," as
Douglas was called, the debates accomplished the great
purpose which Lincoln had in mind. They made clear to

the people the issues involved in the slavery question. They aroused public sentiment. They developed public opinion not only in the State of Illinois but throughout the Union. For newspaper reporters came from as far away as New York, and the reports of these speeches were read everywhere throughout the country. Still more, they drove the South to reject all compromises and insist upon an out-and-out slavery man for President.

Certain it is that they gave Lincoln a prominence outside of his own State that he never had had before. Before the debates began his friends were fearful. Some of them believed that he was putting his head into the lion's mouth and ending his political life. But such was not the case. For, although Douglas became United States senator, Lincoln had given such striking evidence of his breadth, vision, and true statesmanship that two years later he became the choice of the Republican party for President of the United States.

But this was a long look into the future, and he could not foresee that outcome. Now his political horizon loomed dark. Still courage did not forsake him. While he was walking home in the gloom and darkness of that rainy election night, after he had heard of his defeat for the senatorship, he slipped in the muddy street and came near falling to the ground; but on recovering his balance he said to himself, as he thought sadly on the news of his defeat: "It is a slip and not a fall."

For four long years he had struggled manfully to convince the people that slavery was wrong and should not be extended into new States. And to him it appeared that in this great cause he was making but little progress. Yet courage and hope and faith never failed him. "The result is not doubtful," he told his friends. "We shall not fail if we stand firm. We shall not fail. Wise counsels may accelerate or mistakes delay it; but, sooner or later, the victory is sure to come." And so it proved. The present outcome was not final. The day of success was merely postponed.

CHAPTER VII

LINCOLN ELECTED PRESIDENT

THE prominence into which the now famous debates with Douglas brought Lincoln made him a national figure. He received many invitations to speak in various parts of the country, the most important being New York, where he made an address at Cooper Union on February 27, 1860.

Realizing the value of this opportunity, Lincoln prepared his speech with the greatest possible care. His audience was large, cultivated, and brilliant. Among the distinguished men sitting on the platform with him were William Cullen Bryant, who presided, Horace Greeley, and David Dudley Field, all men of national fame.

Lincoln was not insensible to the difference between this group of polished men and those of whom he had formed the centre in the frontier towns of the West. Being a sensitive and discerning man, he must have felt the contrast between himself and them. His personal appearance seldom engaged his thought seriously, but now evidently he became painfully conscious, for a brief interval, of the clothes he wore. Before leaving Springfield he had bought a ready-made suit, which did not fit his gaunt figure—

no ready-made suit ever did. When he took it out of his little valise on reaching New York, it was badly wrinkled. The sleeves were too short for his long arms, and when he stood up to speak, one leg of his trousers caught above his shoe. A smile rippled over the vast audience. Lincoln was plainly embarrassed. His hands trembled, and when about to begin his fourth page he lost his place. After vainly struggling to find it, he put aside his manuscript and continued speaking without it.

Although he had begun in a low, stammering voice, he soon gained self-mastery, and then his forceful arguments, along with his earnest manner, captured his audience, who followed him with rapt interest. In closing this remarkable speech, which held his listeners spellbound for an hour and a half, he said: "Let us have faith that right makes might; and in that faith let us, to the end, dare to do our duty as we understand it."

The intelligent men and women present felt the greatness of the man. They knew that they were listening to a statesman. Next morning Lincoln awoke to find himself famous. "No man," said the New York *Tribune*, "ever before made such an impression on his first appeal to a New York audience." "I do not hesitate to pronounce it," declared Horace Greeley some years later, "the very best political address to which I have ever listened, and I have heard some of Webster's grandest."

Another of his listeners said that after Lincoln "began

Lincoln in February, 1860.
From a photograph by Brady, taken at the time of the Cooper Union speech.

to get into his subject, his face lighted as with an inward fire; the whole man was transfigured. I forgot his clothes, his personal appearance, his individual peculiarities. Presently, forgetting myself, I was on my feet with the rest, yelling like a wild Indian, cheering this wonderful man. In the close part of his argument, you could hear the gentle sizzling of the gas-burners. When he reached a climax the thunders of applause were terrific. It was a great speech."

This speech made a tremendous impression, and it did more than any other one thing to give Abraham Lincoln the nomination, in the following May, for the presidency of the United States.

From New York Lincoln went to New England to visit his son Robert, who was at school in Exeter, New Hampshire. The fame of the Cooper Union speech preceded him, and he received many invitations to speak. His addresses in several New England cities made a deep impression upon the thousands of thoughtful men who heard or read what he said. Before his speech in New York, the mention of Abraham Lincoln as a candidate for the presidency would not have been regarded seriously outside of Illinois, Ohio, Indiana, and Iowa. But the friendly reception given him in New York and in New England encouraged him in his ambition to attain that high office.

Returning to Illinois, Lincoln entered heart and soul into the campaign. Interest in his law practice was absorbed in the greater effort put forth to win the presidency.

Many strong friends came to his support; and he soon had a large following in his own State, where confidence in him had been growing since the time of his joint debates with Douglas in 1858.

It is not surprising, therefore, that at the Illinois convention held at Decatur on May 9, 1860, Lincoln received the enthusiastic indorsement of his State for the presidency. A dramatic moment was given to that meeting when Lincoln's old friend, John Hanks, marched into the wigwam where the convention was held, bearing on his shoulders two historic fence-rails. On these was inscribed: "From a lot made by Abraham Lincoln and John Hanks in the Sangamon bottom in the year 1830." The sight of these rails brought forth loud and prolonged cheers. They were a token of the kinship between these hard-working, rough-visaged men and their gifted brother. It was a glad hour for Lincoln, whose heart beat high with pride at the evidence of their trust and loyal support.

Before the end of that month the Republican National Convention was held in Chicago, in a wigwam built for the occasion and large enough to accommodate ten thousand people.

By the time the four hundred and sixty-five delegates from all over the Union—except nine of the slave States—had arrived, at least forty thousand men had gathered in the city, in order to be present on this important occasion. There were several candidates, the strongest, as most

people believed, being Senator William H. Seward of New
York, a distinguished leader of the Republican party. His
eminence as a statesman, and his ability and experience,
so far overshadowed that of any other candidate that his
nomination seemed almost a certainty. This was true up

The "Wigwam," Chicago, in which the Convention was Held when Lincoln
was Nominated.

to the end of the session of Thursday, the second day. If
the vote had been taken then, Seward would doubtless
have been the winning candidate. The men who were
fighting against him were so sure of this that they secured
an adjournment until Friday morning.

In the hours intervening, the Lincoln managers worked
hard. There was a well-grounded belief that Seward would

be strongly opposed by the men of his party in the doubtful States of Pennsylvania, New Jersey, Indiana, and Illinois, and the Lincoln leaders made use of that fact. They argued: "Seward is too radical for the many conservative voters in these four States. In them he cannot win, and their vote is necessary for the success of the Republican ticket." This was a strong argument, since the success or failure of the presidential candidate in carrying a State greatly influences the election or defeat of the governor and other officers in that State, all being on the same ticket.

The State leaders realized that the new party would probably win or lose in their States according to the popularity of the presidential candidate chosen by the convention. This made the nomination a burning question for themselves as well as for their country. It was a night of thrilling excitement. Party leaders slept little. Their followers hurried hither and yon. Messages flashed back and forth.

Seward's men were confident that he would be nominated on Friday morning. Yet to strengthen his cause they had large bodies of men, accompanied by bands of music and led in cheering by strong-voiced leaders, marching and countermarching through the streets, making noisy demonstrations in his favor. They carried banners and transparencies. They set off rockets, and they serenaded the State delegates whose support they expected to receive. The streets were alive with excitement.

The Lincoln leaders too were organized, and they even outgeneraled the Seward men, as we shall see. They gathered ten thousand men who were ready to do duty for Lincoln—to march for him, shout for him, and if need be fight for him. Lincoln flags were stretched across every street, and Lincoln emblems decorated busses and buildings on every side. But, best of all, next morning at daybreak, while the Seward men were noisily parading the streets, Lincoln's supporters, several thousand strong, were shrewdly securing the best seats in the convention hall, ready to shout, cheer, and break out in deafening applause at every mention of Lincoln's name. Hundreds of women, also, were present; and at every mention of his name they waved handkerchiefs and joined the men in fluttering the many small flags which had been distributed for this special purpose.

Let us imagine ourselves at the convention. We are seated in the great wigwam, facing a huge platform crowded with delegates. The clock is on the stroke of ten, and the presiding officer has risen to open the meeting. The various nominations have been made. Presently the first ballot is taken. Eagerly we await the count. Ah! Seward has 173½; Lincoln, 102; Cameron, 50½; Chase, 49; Bates, 48; scattering, 42; necessary to a choice, 233.

Although Seward has failed by 59½ votes to get the nomination on the first ballot, his followers have lost none of their confidence that he will win. The vast audience is electrified with intense excitement, and all are alert for the trial of strength which is to follow. "Call the roll! Call the roll!" shouts delegate after delegate.

The second ballot stands: Seward, 184½; Lincoln, 181; and all the rest 99½. Seward has gained 11 votes; Lincoln has gained 79. The Seward leaders turn pale, for the vote points unmistakably to the success of Lincoln. With intense interest all follow the third roll-call. The great hall is so still that we can hear the scratching of pencils as men with trembling hands

William H. Seward.

nervously write out the record. When the last State responds, the tally shows that Seward's vote has fallen to 180, while Lincoln's has risen to 231½. Only 1½ more needed for the nomination! But even before the ballot can be announced, four of the Ohio votes are transferred from Chase to Lincoln, and Lincoln has won. The nomination is made unanimous.

Then come such loud shouting and prolonged cheering from the thousands gone mad with enthusiasm, that we can hardly hear the report of the cannon on the roof as it booms the signal to the crowds outside. They take up the sound and pass it on through the city, where bells ring and whistles shriek and blow. Chicago is jubilant. Her favorite has won!

The news spread like wildfire over the prairies and flashed over the wires to the East. When Senator Douglas heard of Lincoln's nomination, he remarked to a group of Republicans at the Capitol: "Gentlemen, you have nominated a very able and a very honest man."

But not to all even of the Republican leaders was the message a pleasing one. It came as a shock to many who had not yet learned to know the sterling qualities of the candidate. Those who had expected the nomination of Seward were startled and alarmed. They declared that the choice of this country lawyer, this inexperienced backwoodsman, as they chose to call him, to be the executive head of a great country like ours, was an appalling blunder.

"I remember," said a Republican of 1860, "that when I first read the news on the bulletin-board I experienced a moment of intense physical pain. It was as though some one had dealt me a heavy blow over the head. Then my strength failed me. I believed our cause was doomed." This is hardly surprising when we remember that until Lincoln entered upon the series of joint debates with Stephen

A. Douglas, only two years before, he was practically unknown outside of his own State.

But where was Lincoln during all this seething turmoil of the convention? In Springfield, waiting quietly and as patiently as possible for the end. It had been to him a most trying week, and under the strain of expectation he had many depressed hours. On the morning when the balloting took place, he said to a friend: "I guess I'll go back to the law business." But he stood with a crowd in front of his office listening to the news as it came over the wire.

When the strain became too great, he suddenly remembered an errand he had promised to do for Mrs. Lincoln across the street. He had made his purchase and stood in the doorway, when a boy from his office came tearing through the crowd with a telegram in his hand. "Mr. Lincoln, Mr. Lincoln, you have received the nomination!" he shouted. There was great general rejoicing, in which Mr. Lincoln joined for a few minutes. Then he said quietly: "There is a little woman down at our house who will like to hear this. I'll go down and tell her"—and he was off in a hasty search for Mrs. Lincoln, to share with her the joy of that happy hour.

Thirty-six hours after Lincoln's nomination in Chicago, a committee of distinguished men stepped off the train at Springfield to notify him of the event. They quietly passed through the streets to the plain, modest, two-story house

where the Lincolns lived in an unfashionable quarter of
the town.

Lincoln received them in his living-room with quiet

Lincoln Receiving News of His Nomination.

dignity.   Already suffering from a reaction which followed
the first good news of his nomination, he was now in a sad
and depressed mood.   While the chairman was speaking
the group of men were giving their candidate a critical sur-

vey. His appearance made a poor impression upon them. His thick, dark hair lay in disorder, his eyes were sombre and downcast, and his stooping shoulders made him appear to be a man without strength of will or definite purpose. But as soon as he began to speak, his body became erect, his eyes lighted up with intelligence and high resolve, and his voice was clear and firm. As he became absorbed in giving his thoughts expression, his personality seemed to undergo a transformation. Thrilled by this sudden and complete change, Lincoln's auditors noted with surprise and pleasure that he was a man of strength, well worthy of their respect and confidence.

His remarks were very brief, but they were in good taste. He expressed his appreciation of the honor he had received, and the sense of the responsibility he must meet. One of the members of the committee, who had voted against Lincoln, turning to Carl Schurz, remarked: "Sir, we might have done a more daring thing, but we certainly could not have done a better thing." And it was with that feeling that the committee, after an hour or so of genial conversation, went away.

Lincoln's formal letter of acceptance, though hardly one hundred and fifty words in length, was prepared with the greatest care. When he had finished it he took it to Dr. Bateman, a friend who was State superintendent of public instruction, for criticism and correction. "Mr. Schoolmaster," said Lincoln, "here is my letter of acceptance. I am not very strong on grammar, and I wish you to see if it is all right; I shouldn't like to have any mistakes in it."

After reading the manuscript Dr. Bateman said: "There is only one change I should suggest, Mr. Lincoln.

Lincoln's Home, Springfield.

You have written, 'It shall be my care *to not violate* or disregard it in any part.' You should have written *'not to violate.'* Never split an infinitive, is the rule."

Mr. Lincoln, after looking at the manuscript thoughtfully, remarked, as he made the change: "So you think I better put those two little fellows end to end, do you?"

The nomination having been made, the party press, the Republican organization, rival candidates, and literary men all united in the support of the candidate. From the day of his nomination till his election, steady and earnest work for the ticket went on. This heartened Lincoln, who after the first joy of his success began to feel the burden of his responsibility. Street parades of young men calling themselves "Wide Awakes," dressed in black oilcloth capes and hats, carrying flaming torches, singing campaign songs, and bearing aloft banners and transparencies, added to the interest and excitement of the campaign.

There was the stumping of the country by eminent campaign speakers. Pamphlets and campaign tracts were freely scattered. Many of the people who did not know Lincoln before, learned to respect and trust him from his printed speeches. In these ways a great education went on, and much enthusiasm was created. Before the close of the campaign, the voters in Lincoln's own and neighboring States formed a procession eight miles long and marched past his house. With friends he sat upon his piazza, answering the salutes in his friendly way.

As his custom was, Lincoln continued to live a very simple life. Every day up to the time of his nomination, he had gone, after closing his office, out on the common and driven home his cow, fed and groomed his horse, cleaned out his humble stable, and then chopped wood and carried it in for the kitchen fire. After his nomination there was little change in these simple, homely habits. But it seemed to his friends that neither his home nor his dingy law office was an appropriate place to meet the visitors that came in throngs to see him. So an office was secured in the State

House, which stood on the village green in the centre of the town. Every morning about eight o'clock Lincoln was at his desk; but on his way there, as in previous years, he liked to stop and talk with his friends.

Lincoln Office in the State-House, Occupied after the Nomination.

Of course his visitors were numerous. On some days the throng was so great that he could not attend to the letters that came to him in ever-increasing numbers. But no matter how crowded his office, nor how high his desk might be piled up with important mail, he never lost his patience and never seemed to be in a hurry.

Many of his visitors were eminent men; but some were the backwoods people he had known years before, when he kept store in New Salem or when he was surveying in

Sangamon County. On one occasion, while he was receiving some distinguished political leaders from a distance, an elderly woman in a big sunbonnet, coarse shoes, and a short dress appeared, carrying in her hand a package wrapped in brown paper and tied with a white string. Lincoln turned at once to greet her, inquiring for her "folks." Handing him the package, which contained a pair of coarse blue woollen stockings, she said with pride: "I wanted to give you somethin', Mr. Linkin, to take to Washington, and that's all I had. I spun that yarn and knit them socks myself."

After thanking her heartily Lincoln escorted her to the door with as much courtesy as if she had been a queen, and then going back to the visitors, he picked up the stockings and holding them by the toes, one in each hand, he remarked with a whimsical smile: "The old lady got my latitude and longitude about right, didn't she?" Such incidents, showing the friendly attitude of the plain people toward the man who had worked humbly among them, were frequent and gave Lincoln much pleasure.

On election day the townspeople crowded into the office in larger numbers than usual. Observing this, some one suggested that Lincoln should close the office-door in order to have command of his time. But he said: "I have never yet closed my doors against my friends, and I shall not do so to-day."

After Lincoln's nomination the country grew more and

more excited over the slavery question. What the South
would do was doubtful. When the Democratic convention met in June, the Southern members wished that there
should be inserted in the platform of the party a plank
clearly stating that slavery should exist in the Territories
without interference on the part of Congressional or Territorial legislation. To this the Northern Democrats would
not agree. They insisted that Douglas's policy of popular
sovereignty ought to be carried out in the Territories.

Douglas, you will remember, in answer to Lincoln's
question in their debate about the matter, had said that
the people of any Territory could by unfriendly legislation
put an end to slavery within their borders. That answer
was the rock on which his ship had foundered; for, as Lincoln's clear vision had foreseen, it aroused hostile criticism
in the South and Douglas lost his hold there. This led to
a split in the Democratic party. The Northern Democrats
nominated Douglas for President, while the Southern Democrats nominated John C. Breckinridge.

Since the Democratic vote would be divided between the
two candidates, neither could win without getting many
votes from the Republican party. Would the Republicans
stand by Lincoln? That was the pressing question.

During the trying period between Lincoln's nomination
in May and the presidential election in November, he refused to say anything as to his future policy. He would
grant no interviews to newspaper men, make no speeches,

and write no letters for the public to read. He wisely said it would be useless for him to announce his views on political questions, because he had clearly set them forth in his speeches and he had not changed his mind. During the entire campaign he remained in Springfield, and he made but one speech. This was on the evening following his nomination, when the townspeople in serenading him asked him to address them. At that time he said that, as to his position on the political questions of the day, he could only refer them to his previous speeches. He then added: "Fellow citizens and friends, the time comes upon every public man when it is best for him to keep his lips closed. That time has come upon me."

There were especially good reasons why he should choose to remain silent. The South was seething with excitement over his nomination, and to keep saying the same things that had aroused their fears and perhaps their hatred could only add to the bad feeling in the South, without further enlightening or convincing the North.

The results of election day in November witnessed in no uncertain way to the people's faith in Lincoln, for out of 303 electoral votes he received 180.

The South now became tense with excitement. Threats of secession had been made for some time, and when Lincoln was elected South Carolina at once seceded. The politicians of that State had never forgotten his bitter opposition to slavery, nor his speech declaring that a house divided against itself could not stand. They looked upon the President-elect as a menace to the existence of slavery, and chose to protect themselves by setting up a government of their own.

In the midst of all the turmoil and confusion of the hour, those newspapers hostile to Lincoln said that there ought to be some compromise offered which would-allay excitement and stop secession. Some of the Republican papers, also, joined in this demand. It was as if they thought Lincoln's election had caused all the trouble and that therefore it was Lincoln's duty to stop it. Among other appeals Lincoln received one from John A. Gilmer, a congressman from North Carolina, who earnestly desired that the Union should be preserved and begged Lincoln to do something. In answer Lincoln wrote as follows:

"I have not thought of recommending the abolition of slavery in the District of Columbia nor the slave-trade among the slave States; and if I should make such a recommendation it is quite clear Congress would not follow it. On the Territorial question I am inflexible. . . . On that there is a difference between you and us; and it is the only substantial difference. You think slavery is right and ought to be extended; we think it wrong and ought to be restricted. For this neither has just cause to be angry with the other."

Again, a week later, Lincoln wrote to Alexander H. Stephens, of Georgia, whom he had known in Congress and who afterward became vice-president of the Southern Confederacy. This is a part of the letter which he marked "For your eyes only":

"Do the people of the South really entertain fears that a Republican administration would directly or indirectly interfere with the slaves? If they do, I wish to assure you, as once a friend, and still, I hope, not an enemy, that there is no cause for such fears. The South would be in no more danger in this respect than in the days of Washington. I suppose, however, that this does not meet the case. You think slavery is right and ought to be extended, while we think it is wrong and ought to be restricted. That, I suppose, is the rub. It certainly is the only substantial difference between us."

Not all of the people in the Southern States believed in secession. Many leading men, both North and South, sought some plan by which it might be avoided. Secession, they believed, would lead to coercion, and coercion would lead to bloodshed. There was on both sides a strong desire that the trouble might be settled.

One of the plans discussed was an amendment to the Constitution. The originator of this plan was Senator Crittenden, of Kentucky. He proposed to Congress a compromise which provided that the parallel of thirty-six degrees thirty minutes north latitude—the Missouri Compromise line—should be the separating line between free territory and slave territory as far as the Pacific coast.

But Lincoln was inflexible about the extension of slavery, and wrote to Mr. Kellogg, of Illinois, a member of the committee chosen to consider the Crittenden Compromise: "Entertain no proposition for a compromise in regard to the extension of slavery. The instant you do they have us under again. All our labor is lost and sooner or later must be done over. . . . The tug has to come and better now than later." A less courageous man than Lincoln might have sought shelter in compromise from the destructive storm which he foresaw was about to break upon his administration.

Further evidence of his determination to face the issue squarely appears in a letter he wrote in December to his friend, E. B. Washburne, who had just given him a report of a conference with General Scott, commander-in-chief of the army, upon the danger threatening the country. "Please present my respects to the general," Lincoln wrote, "and tell him, confidentially, that I shall be obliged to him to be as well prepared as he can either to hold or retake the forts, as the case may require, at or after the inauguration."

These letters show that although Lincoln was making no speeches and no public appeals of any kind, yet he was not inactive. On the contrary, he was thoroughly alive to what was going on, and was doing all that was possible for a man in his position to do to prepare for the terrible catastrophe which he saw inevitably advancing. He was also meeting in Springfield many Republican leaders, some of whom were presenting various plans to calm the distracted people. But Lincoln could do little as yet. Four months intervened before he would come into office.

Buchanan, who was then President of the United States, had a great opportunity, but he did not use it. "He seemed at that time," said Crittenden, of whom we have just spoken, "shaken in body and uncertain in mind—an old man worn by worry." He had almost lost the power of making any definite decision. In his annual message to Congress, December 4, 1860, he denied the right of any State to secede, but a little further on in his message he declared that Congress had no power to coerce a State if it did secede. When the country needed a strong hand at the helm, Buchanan allowed things to drift, and the worst of it was that they were drifting away from the government. In spite of his weakness and vacillation, however, the common belief now is that he was sincere, honest, and patriotic. The fact is, he was in a most painful and even pitiful situation, for which he had to thank largely his own past course as a pro-slavery advocate ready to do the bidding of the Southern leaders.

To make matters worse, there was division of opinion in Lincoln's own party as to how secession should be dealt with. Horace Greeley, editor of the New York *Tribune*, who at that time was one of the foremost leaders in the Republican party, said in the editorial columns of his paper on November 9, 1860: "If the cotton States shall decide that they can do better out of the Union than in it, we insist on letting them go in peace." This was a shocking blow to the Union cause.

On December 17 he again said through the editorial columns of the *Tribune* that the South had as good a right to secede from the Union as the colonists had to secede from Great Britain in the days of the American Revolution; and as late as February 26, only a week before Lincoln's inauguration, Greeley declared, in words that startled many loyal Union men, that if the cotton States, or the Gulf States, chose to form an independent nation they had a clear moral right to do so.

Thurlow Weed, editor of the Albany *Evening Journal* and a close friend of William H. Seward, declared himself in favor of making concessions to the South, even expressing the wish that the Republicans might "meet secession as patriots and not as partisans."

Henry Ward Beecher, a Brooklyn clergyman of powerful eloquence, when asked whether he thought the South would secede, replied: "I don't believe they will, and I don't care if they do." And the business men of the North, almost stampeded by the prospect of confusion and chaos in industry and commerce, became strongly desirous that steps be taken in the direction of concession, compromise, or even surrender to the demands of the Southern slaveholders.

To many the country seemed to be moving toward ruin. There was general alarm. The situation had become more than dangerous—it was appalling. All seemed powerless to avert the threatening disaster.

But the people's chosen leader, Abraham Lincoln, calm and cool-headed, never wavered. He absolutely refused to yield to any plan of compromise on the fundamental doctrine of the Republican party. "There must be no extension of slavery," he said; "we must keep the evil institution where it is."

In the midst of all this distraction and confusion Lincoln, about the middle of January, 1861, set about preparing his inaugural address. He wrote it in an up-stairs back room of the building in which he had his law office. It was a dingy room containing one chair and an old desk provided with an inkstand and a steel pen. For references he had only the Constitution, Jackson's "Nullification Proclamation," Webster's "Reply to Hayne," and Henry Clay's speech of 1850. With these few helps and in these bare surroundings Abraham Lincoln, alone with his own spirit, prepared what is now considered a famous state paper, his first inaugural.

Having finished this task, he began, about two weeks before leaving Springfield, to put his business in order. One of the things he did was to visit his aged stepmother in Coles County. He wished to spend a day with her and go to his father's grave. She had been good to him when he was a motherless boy, and he had always been good to her since the day when he left his father's home to fight life's battles for himself. Now, before taking up his work as President, he wished to make provision for her comfort

Sarah Bush Lincoln.

while he should be far away from her. But her thought was more for him than for herself, and she broke into sobs as she told him her fear that his life would be taken by the hands of a murderer, and that she should never see him again. Many friends, among them Hannah Armstrong, shared this fear, for his life had been often threatened. His farewell visit to his old law partner, Herndon, gives another interesting glimpse of this great man. After taking care of some business details Lincoln crossed the room and lay down upon the old sofa, which was so familiar to him. For a few moments he looked up at the ceiling without speaking a word. Then, turning to his partner, he said gently:

"Billy, how long have we been together?"

"Over sixteen years," was the answer.

"We have never had a cross word during all that time, have we?"

Before bidding farewell to his partner he turned to him and said: "I wish the sign to remain as it is. Let it hang there undisturbed. . . . If I live I am coming back sometime and then we will go right on practising law as if nothing had happened." Then, tying up some books and papers, he went out of the office, never to return.

In the meanwhile the determination of the Southern States to set up a government of their own was being actually carried out. For by February 1 six other cotton States—Mississippi, Florida, Alabama, Georgia, Louisiana, and Texas—had joined South Carolina in seceding from the Union. Delegates from these seven States met at Montgomery, Alabama, on February 9, and organized the Southern Confederacy. They agreed upon a constitution and elected Jefferson Davis President, and Alexander H. Stephens Vice-President. At first the Confederate capital was Montgomery, but later it was made Richmond, Virginia.

Lincoln was to be inaugurated on March 4. On the morning of February 11, the day before his fifty-second birthday, with his family and a few personal friends he started for Washington. It was a few minutes before eight o'clock when he made his way out of the waiting-room of

the Springfield railroad-station through a throng of friends
and neighbors who were gathered to say good-by. Having
reached his special car, he took his place on the rear platform. As he looked down upon the kindly, upturned faces
of those who knew and loved him, a wave of emotion swept
over his tall figure. His lips quivered, and tears filled his
eyes. For a few moments he stood in solemn silence. Then,
getting control of himself, he spoke in a husky voice the
following sad farewell:

"My friends, no one not in my situation can appreciate my feeling of sadness at this parting. To this place
and the kindness of these people I owe everything. Here
I have lived a quarter of a century, and have passed from a
young to an old man. Here my children have been born
and one is buried. I now leave, not knowing when or
whether ever I may return, with a task before me greater
than that which rested on Washington. Without the assistance of that Divine Being who ever attended him I
cannot succeed; with that assistance I cannot fail. Trust-
ing in him who can go with me and remain with you and
be everywhere for good, let us confidently hope that all
will yet be well. To his care commending you, as I hope
in your prayers you will commend me, I bid you an affectionate farewell."

When he said that with the help of God he could not
fail, there was vigorous applause; and when, with deep
emotion, he appealed to his friends and neighbors for their

prayers, with sobbing voices they cried out: "We will do it! We will do it!" During his speech, even though the snow was falling fast, every hat was lifted and every head eagerly bent forward to catch his words.

As the train moved off, Lincoln's friends watched him standing on the platform and taking his last look at the town where he had spent so much of his life.

The journey to Washington occupied twelve days, and was crowded with interesting and dramatic incidents. There was great enthusiasm all along the way. Through the long stretches of scattered villages and towns, people gathered as the train whirled on, cheering, waving handkerchiefs, and tossing hats into the air. Wherever there were stops, men and women crowded to shake hands with Mr. Lincoln, and at the large centres of Indianapolis, Cincinnati, Columbus, and Pittsburgh, formal entertainments were arranged and speeches were made. The presidential party was constantly enlivened along the route by delegations of leading citizens, who came ahead to escort the party to their respective cities. In this way the company was constantly changing.

Lincoln took three days to get through New York State, stopping for elaborate ceremonies in Albany and New York City. All along the Eastern route there were the same crowds as in the West, with booming cannon, gifts of flowers, receptions, dinners, and luncheons with the prominent officials. Flags, banners, and mottoes all bore their part in giving a welcome to the President-elect. During this joyous progress Lincoln made thirty speeches, which were received with enthusiasm by those who listened to them and with strained attention by the press of the country.

To many, however, they were a keen disappointment. As you will recall, during all the period that had elapsed between his nomination and his leaving Springfield he had remained silent about his policies. The people expected now that he would have something to say about the events that were distracting the country and the measures with which he would meet them. To many of them his speeches seemed to be feeble and overcautious, and to indicate his unfitness for the great task awaiting him. Some wished to hear his future policy outlined in vigorous tones.

The press was especially unfriendly in quoting from some of his speeches such words as the following: (At Columbus) "It is a good thing that there is not more than anxiety, for there is nothing going wrong. It is a consoling circumstance that when we look out, there is nothing that really hurts anybody." (At Pittsburgh) "In plain words, there is really no crisis except an artificial one." (At Cleveland) "I think there is no occasion for any excitement. . . . As I said before, this crisis is all artificial! It has no foundation in fact. Let it alone, and it will go down itself."

These remarks, made by the man who was soon to become President of the United States, led the people to think that he did not realize the gravity of the situation. But they were mistaken. Separated from the rest of the speech, these quotations had not exactly the same meaning as in their proper setting. The President-elect did realize his difficulties and the dangers to the country, but he did not wish unduly to stir up the people by dwelling upon them. Besides, the time was not ripe to declare the sentiments which he wished to state in his inaugural speech, and it did not seem prudent to announce his policy until he had received control of the government.

Jefferson Davis.

Notwithstanding the criticism of Mr. Lincoln's speeches, however, the common people continued to greet him with glowing enthusiasm all along the way, and the journey was a joyful one until a rumor came that there was a plot to assassinate him when he passed through Baltimore.

When Lincoln and his party reached Philadelphia, the noted detective, Allan Pinkerton, who had been brought along by Mr. Lincoln's friends, declared that there was good evidence of such a plot.   The same rumor was brought by Seward's son, who had been sent by his father from Washington to Philadelphia, to warn Mr. Lincoln.

At first Lincoln refused to yield to those who advised him to change his plans in the interest of his personal safety; but finally he said he would consider the matter, although he would not allow it to interfere with his engagements.   According to his original schedule, therefore he attended a flag-raising at Independence Hall, in Philadelphia, early on the morning of February 22, and then went on to Harrisburg to address the Pennsylvania legislature in the afternoon.   On the following day, according to the original plan, he was to return to Philadelphia, and there take a train through Baltimore to Washington.

But in Harrisburg, to avoid needless risk, he decided to go through Baltimore that night.   So at six o'clock on the evening of the 22d he left the dining-room of the hotel and went to his apartments, where he put on a travelling-suit. His wife begged to go with him and share his danger, but that did not seem wise, and he was obliged to leave her sobbing in fear that his life might be taken.   Going out by a back way with his old friend, Ward H. Lamon, who used to ride the circuit with him in Illinois, he entered a carriage belonging to the governor of Pennsylvania, and was driven to the railroad-station, where the two boarded a special train, and were soon speeding away toward Philadelphia, there to take the regular train for Washington. Mr. Lincoln quietly entered his sleeping-car and went to his section unnoticed. About six o'clock the next morning they were in Washington, where Mr. Seward and Mr. Washburne met them.

There is no proof that a plot had been laid to assassinate Mr. Lincoln, but we cannot doubt his wisdom in taking every precaution in the face of what then seemed a real danger to his life. It would have been an irreparable national calamity if he had been assassinated at that time.

Lincoln had nine days in Washington

Mary Todd Lincoln.

before his inauguration, days filled with pressing business, official visits and visitors, conferences with his future cabinet members, and countless other matters.

The 4th of March, 1861, the day of his inauguration, was bright and sunny. At the appointed hour a Senate committee with President Buchanan went to Willard's

Hotel, where Mr. Lincoln was awaiting them. They drove to the Capitol in a barouche drawn by six horses. Both sides of their route were flanked by veteran soldiers, heavily armed, to prevent any possible interference with the inauguration, for there were heard predictions that Lincoln would never become President.

The inaugural ceremonies took place on a platform erected at the east portico of the Capitol. When Lincoln stepped out on the platform to begin his address, the cheering from an audience which was more curious than friendly was only half-hearted. He carried in one hand a gold-headed cane and in the other a new silk hat. The cane he put in a corner, and in some embarrassment looked for a place to put his hat, for he did not wish to lay it down on the floor. While Lincoln stood as if uncertain what to do, and the immense throng were watching him curiously, his old rival, Stephen A. Douglas, who was standing just behind him, reached out his hand for the hat and held it while Lincoln took the oath of office and delivered his inaugural.

As Douglas was helping Lincoln out of his difficulty, he smilingly whispered to one of Lincoln's friends: "If I cannot be President, I can at least hold his hat." Douglas had said in the earlier part of the day that he meant to put himself as prominently forward as he properly could, in order to make it clear to all, Northerners and Southerners alike, that he would use all his strength and ability to support the new administration in what it might do to save the Union. This simple and friendly action on the part of the patriotic leader of the Northern Democrats attracted much attention.

"Mr. Lincoln read his inaugural," said Mr. Herndon, "in a clear, distinct, and musical voice, which seemed to be heard and distinctly understood on the very outskirts of the vast concourse of his fellow citizens."

In the course of this inaugural, which is now famous, he declared that no State upon its own motion could lawfully go out of the Union, and that to the extent of his ability he would take care, as the Constitution itself expressly enjoined upon him, that the laws of the Union be faithfully executed in all the States. He closed with the following beautiful and impressive words:

"I am loath to close. We are not enemies but friends. We must not be enemies. Though passion may have strained, it must not break, our bonds of affection. The mystic chords of memory, stretching from every battle-field and patriot grave to every living heart and hearthstone all over this broad land, will yet swell the chorus of the Union when again touched, as surely they will be, by the better angels of our nature."

To the surprise of many, Lincoln said nothing about slavery. He was wise in omitting mention of this great issue, for another and more momentous one was now before the country and claimed first attention. That was the preservation of the Union. It was upon that issue that Lincoln laid emphasis, not so much with the expectation of influencing the South as with the hope of effecting a united North and cementing to the Union the powerful border States, which it was so necessary that he should keep loyal. The most important of these States were Maryland, Kentucky, and Missouri. This emphasis upon the preservation of the Union rather than upon any phase of the slavery question gives evidence to-day of Lincoln's remarkable vision and practical wisdom as a statesman.

The oath of office was administered by Chief Justice Taney, and immediately batteries of guns fired a national salute to the chief. Lincoln was then escorted by Buchanan, through the multitudes of people, to the executive mansion.

CHAPTER VIII

LONELY DAYS IN THE WHITE HOUSE

FATEFUL crossing of a threshold! The oath had committed the country to Lincoln's keeping, and he would carry the load even at the sacrifice of his own life. The people had chosen better than they knew; but let us see with what sort of welcome they cheered their leader, and what support they held out to make his burden less heavy.

We are already aware that he was little known at the time of his nomination; that during the four months of the campaign which followed he took no active part, so far as his countrymen could learn, in what was going on. We know that many thought that his speeches, during his two weeks' journey to Washington just before his inauguration, lacked boldness, vigor, and breadth, and failed to indicate a clear grasp of the perilous situation. To their minds, the man who had become the executive head of the nation was unfit for his great task.

Such a feeling was not unnatural in those who did not know the man, for Abraham Lincoln had been brought up in the backwoods in the midst of poverty and ignorance. He himself said that he had never gone to school a year in his life. He was also untrained and untried. The only executive position he had ever filled was that of postmaster in

143

the little village of New Salem. Certainly the Republican party was thrusting a rash experiment upon the country in making such a man the national leader in a time of so great a crisis. The country was on the verge of civil war. That Abraham Lincoln, the rail-splitter and country lawyer, who had thus far been successful mainly as a clever politician and a stump speaker, was to become by his patience, courage, judgment, high purpose, unselfishness, and strength of will the successful leader of the nation through this great crisis, nobody could know. To his excited critics it even appeared foolhardy in him to be willing to assume such a responsibility.

Even in his own party the majority of the political leaders held this view when he became President. They had not yet found out for themselves what a Southerner had said in February, 1861—that Abraham Lincoln would do his own thinking.

Nor did the members of his Cabinet know him any better. Among these men who were to sit at his council-table and advise him as to what was wise to do were four men—Seward, Chase, Bates, and Cameron—who had been his rivals for the presidency. Some of his friends doubted the wisdom of his appointing so many men who had been his own rivals and rivals of one another. They predicted trouble in bringing about the harmonious action that was absolutely necessary. But Lincoln answered: "No, gentlemen, the times are too grave and perilous for ambitious

Lincoln in 1861.
From a photograph owned by Allen Jasper Conant.

145

schemes and personal rivalries. I need the aid of all these men. They enjoy the confidence of their several States and sections, and they will strengthen the administration."

It was not of himself but of the best interests of the country that he was constantly thinking. Since his supreme ambition was to give his best service, he sought, in making appointments to his Cabinet, the ablest men, and personal feeling did not enter into the matter. Edwin M. Stanton, who had violently abused him during the first part of his administration, he later nominated as secretary of war. Lincoln apparently never gave Stanton's criticism serious thought, for he believed that Stanton, better than any one else, could fill that important position. Guided, as always, by impersonal motives, he chose a Cabinet among whose members there was not a single personal friend, not one whom he had known for a year. This meant that there was no understanding mind, no friendly heart in which he could confide, and that the burden of his decisions he must carry alone.

As many of the Cabinet members were men of very much wider experience in public life than the President, it was natural that they should feel superior to him. This was especially true of William H. Seward, secretary of state, and Salmon P. Chase, secretary of the treasury. As a matter of fact, one of the delicate and trying tasks which lay before Mr. Lincoln was to show these two men that they were in reality as in name his secretaries, and that he was in reality as in name their official chief.

Seward was the first of all the Cabinet to learn with something of a shock that Lincoln was to be the ruling

Edwin M. Stanton.

mind in the new administration. It seems clear that at the start he regarded Lincoln as unfit for his high office, and believed that he himself, as occupying the first place in the Cabinet, and as the most powerful leader in the Republican party, must save the country if it was to be saved at all. Certainly, from his point of view, the President was too ignorant and weak to do it. So at first Seward opposed the holding of any Cabinet meetings, and the President yielded. Then it was planned to have a meeting on Tuesdays and Fridays, but Seward let it be understood that no member should be present unless he were notified by the President or himself. Thus it would be brought about that only those whom Seward desired would be present, and he would hold the dominating influence.

In the meantime Lincoln was doing his own thinking and reaching his own decisions, some of which were not in accord with those of his secretary of state; but Seward did not seem to realize this clearly. His belief that Lincoln was incapable of administering the affairs of the nation reached a climax about a month after the inauguration. About April 1 he suggested in writing that the President allow him to take control of the government in order to save the country. It was a high-handed attitude to assume, and a mortal insult to Lincoln.

In his letter to the President Seward said: "We are at the end of a month's administration, and are yet without a policy either domestic or foreign." Then, after suggesting some other courses of action which might be followed to advantage, he continued: "But whatever policy we adopt there must be an energetic prosecution of it. For this purpose it must be somebody's business to pursue and direct it incessantly. Either the President must do it himself and be all the while active in it; or devolve it upon some member of his Cabinet. Once adopted, debates on it must

end and all agree to abide by it.   It is not my special prov-
ince, but I neither seek to evade nor to assume responsibility."

It would not be easy to imagine the feelings of the
President when he read the outrageous suggestion that he
turn over the control of the government to his secretary of
state.   If Seward, occupying the first place in the Cabinet,
and therefore having the best chance to know him, had
such an opinion of the weakness of his chief, what must be
the views of the other Cabinet members?   What must be
the views of the leaders of public opinion in general?

But Lincoln felt no hesitation as to how he should reply
to Seward.   Although modest, he was never self-distrustful.
Even in the troubled days to follow, he had always the
strength of a quiet confidence in himself.   On the day
that Seward's note reached him he sent his answer.   This
was tactful, kind, and firm, but there was no doubt as to
its meaning.   "Upon your closing proposition," he wrote,
"that 'Whatever policy we adopt there must be an energetic prosecution of it.   For this purpose it must be somebody's business to pursue and direct it incessantly.   Either
the President must do it himself, or devolve it on some
member of his Cabinet'—I remark that if this must be
done, I must do it.   When a general line of policy is adopted,
I apprehend there is no danger of its being changed without
good reason, or continuing to be a subject of unnecessary
debate; still, upon points arising in its progress, I wish, and

I am entitled to have, the advice of all the Cabinet." the letter said: "As President of the United States, ... to do and no one else can do it for me." ... as has been learned, this affair never reached the ... other member of Lincoln's Cabinet, or even the ... of his friends. Only his private secretary, ... knew anything about it. It no doubt ... Seward how serious a fault he had com... gave him a new insight into the character ... from that day he became a loyal and de... the President, and brought, in unstinted ... energy and wide influence to the sup...

... knowledge of Lincoln it is difficult to under... could have made so stupendous a blunder; ... patriotic, and he was only a conspicu... many other men in public life thought ... he quickly and completely altered his ... a letter written two months later to ... declared: "Executive force and vigor ... The President is the best of us."

... Lincoln became President, an occa... best to make a decision contrary ... high in office. It concerned Fort ... which was in Charleston harbor, was ... States which the Confederates

pied it. The day when D——————

suppose I am entitled to have, the advice of all the Cabinet."
In effect this letter said: "As President of the United States,
I have a work to do and no one else can do it for me."

So far as has been learned, this affair never reached the
ears of any other member of Lincoln's Cabinet, or even the
most intimate of his friends. Only his private secretary,
John G. Nicolay, knew anything about it. It no doubt
showed Secretary Seward how serious a fault he had committed, and it gave him a new insight into the character
of his chief. From that day he became a loyal and devoted follower of the President, and brought, in unstinted
measure, his tireless energy and wide influence to the support of Lincoln.

With our knowledge of Lincoln it is difficult to understand how Seward could have made so stupendous a blunder;
but his purpose was patriotic, and he was only a conspicuous example of what many other men in public life thought
at that time. That he quickly and completely altered his
judgment is shown in a letter written two months later to
his wife, in which he declared: "Executive force and vigor
are rare qualities. The President is the best of us."

Immediately after Lincoln became President, an occasion arose when he thought best to make a decision contrary
to the advice of those high in office. It concerned Fort
Sumter. This fort, which was in Charleston harbor, was
one of the few in the seceded States which the Confederates
had not seized in February. A small force of less than one

hundred men, under the command of Major Anderson, occupied it.   The day after his inauguration, March 5, Lincoln

Lincoln and His Secretaries, Nicolay and Hay.

had received a request from Major Anderson for food.
There was enough to last only four weeks.   Lincoln immediately consulted General Scott, who thought it would be

impossible, with the means at his command, to comply. Most of the members of his Cabinet, including Seward, advised against it. But to Lincoln's mind there was only one thing to do. The policy of holding or retaking the forts had been plainly set forth in his inaugural, and he did not propose to go back on his word. An expedition with food was sent, and the governor of South Carolina was informed that it carried food alone. This assurance was sent to avoid any possible misunderstanding as to hostile intent, for the President was loath to start an open rupture with the seceded States.

The Confederates, however, restless under inaction and determined that Fort Sumter should not be even provisioned, attacked the fort with several thousand troops. Before the Union fleet could arrive, in the early morning of April 12, the firing began and continued for thirty-four hours.

At last the wooden barracks were set on fire by hot shot. The flames spread beyond control. The heat and smoke drove the men in the garrison to lie flat on the ground, with wet cloths on their mouths, to keep from suffocating. With food and powder almost gone and flag-staff shot away, the garrison had to surrender. The Confederates, admiring the courage of this handful of men, allowed them to retire from the fort, bearing their arms. Just before leaving they fired a salute of fifty guns, and marched out with colors flying and the band playing

"Yankee Doodle."   It was thus that the first shots of the Civil War were exchanged.

The firing upon Fort Sumter startled the nation.   It was the beginning of war, of what might prove to be a long

Interior of Fort Sumter after the Bombardment.

and bloody war.   President Lincoln acted with promptness and decision by calling for seventy-five thousand men and appealing to all loyal citizens for support.   He declared the South under blockade.

For the moment all differences of opinion were smothered in a great wave of patriotism; and the people of the North, united by a deep desire to preserve the Union, responded to the call of their President with genuine enthusiasm.

Money, credit, supplies of all sorts were offered the government.

Both North and South began rapidly to organize armies for the bitter conflict which now seemed inevitable. Several slave States, including the border States, refused to respond to Lincoln. Virginia, North Carolina, Tennessee, and Arkansas seceded. The hostile lines were close to the borders of Washington. There was general alarm. Mothers and children were leaving the city. Mrs. Lincoln was urged to go. "No," she replied, "I am as safe as Mr. Lincoln, and I shall not leave him." Then the troops arrived, and Washington was safe.

In their eagerness to attack, the people grew impatient, but the raw troops had to be drilled and made ready. To this task, before July 1, General McDowell was appointed, being put at the head of the Union army gathered in and about Washington. The Confederate army, under General Beauregard, was stationed around Manassas, near Bull Run, about thirty-five miles away, within easy striking distance. Daily the clamor of the North grew stronger for a march to the Confederate capital. "On to Richmond!" was the loud outcry of the people. Still General Scott and other Union generals insisted that the army was not ready. But at last Lincoln, yielding to the urgent demand of the country, ordered that the advance be made.

On the day of the battle of Bull Run (July 21, 1861) McDowell's army at first drove back the Confederates.

But during their retreat word came that the Southern army was reinforced.   This news, which came about four o'clock in the afternoon, brought panic to the Union army. A stampede followed, which soon became a rout.   Men fled for their lives.   Teamsters cut their traces and rode

Ruins of Stone Bridge, Where the Bull Run Stampede Took Place.

away on their horses.   Soldiers flung aside their muskets and knapsacks and ran.   The army became a mob.

Deep gloom settled over Washington that night, for the defeat was a great blow to the Union cause.   It fell with cruel severity upon President Lincoln.   The early news of the battle had been hopeful, and he was expecting a victory. So, believing that all was going well, he had dropped his work and gone for his afternoon drive.   Imagine the shock of receiving on his return the message: "General McDowell's army in full retreat from Centreville. The day is lost. Save Washington and the remnants of this army." It was feared that the Confederates would attack Washington before morning. Through the drizzling rain crowds of soldiers, negroes, and terrified horses came fleeing into the city, increasing the horror of the situation.

Although the lonely man of the White House suffered keenly in this bitter trial, he remained calm and composed. In the sleepless night following this battle his busy mind was working out plans by which to retrieve the disaster. With all his heart he pitied the young, untried soldiers who had failed to stand under the terrible fire of their first battle, and on Tuesday he found time to visit the camp lying south of the Potomac. There he spoke with tender feeling and encouragement to the "boys in blue," who two days before had fled, panic-stricken, from the battle-field of Bull Run.

This defeat was actually more wholesome for the North than was the victory for the South. For the South was overconfident. Many Southern soldiers began to return to their homes as if the war were over. But that was a great mistake. It had only just begun. In the North the people were nerved to greater energy, for it was clear now that the issue could be settled only by war. The day following the battle, Congress, standing back of the President, voted to raise an army of five hundred thousand men.

Not only did troubles within the country weigh heavily upon the President, but international complications also arose. The "Trent Affair" was a difficulty coming out of the unwarranted action upon the high seas of a Union navy officer. The trouble, briefly stated, was this: To secure aid for the Southern cause, two envoys, Mason and Slidell,

Long Bridge, Washington, over Which the Troops Ran Panic-Stricken from the Battle-Field of Bull Run

had been sent by the Confederate government as commissioners to England and France. They eluded the blockade at Charleston and took passage at Havana on the British mail-steamer Trent. Captain Wilkes, of the United States war-vessel San Jacinto, stopped the Trent off the Bahama Islands (November 8, 1861), took off Mason and Slidell, and later confined them in Fort Warren in Boston harbor.

For this act Captain Wilkes was warmly applauded by the Northern people, who looked upon him as a national hero. The secretary of the navy sent him a letter of congratulation, the secretary of war openly praised him, and the House of Representatives passed a unanimous vote of thanks to him. But England was highly indignant and at once began to make preparations for war. She sent troops and war-vessels to Canada, and with unnecessary earnestness demanded that the prisoners be given up.

When the capture of Mason and Slidell was reported to President Lincoln, he at once declared that "it did not look right for Captain Wilkes to stop the vessel of a friendly power on the high seas, and take out of her, by force, passengers who went on board in one neutral port to be carried to another." Although he would have liked to uphold Wilkes, Secretary Seward, an expert in international law, reassured him in his first impression by telling him that we had always contended against England for the very principle which had been violated by the captain, and that by refusing to come to a satisfactory agreement with England, we should bring on war with that country.

Lincoln, with his strong common sense and his clear ideas of international right and justice, found it easy to reach a wise decision. He gave up the prisoners to England, with the statement that Captain Wilkes had acted without the authority of the United States. This was not only high statesmanship but added greatly to his personal fame. He had the responsibility for these momentous decisions, and he rightly has the credit for them. Throughout the war he was a master in dealing with complex international affairs.

The Trent Affair was but one of the many troubles which gathered thick and fast about Lincoln in his management of the terrible Civil War; and there must have been many times when he longed for a closer companionship in carrying the heavy responsibilities of these distracting first months in the White House, many times when his soul cried out in its loneliness.

Then, while public cares were so exacting and public criticism so scorching, Lincoln had also a very heavy personal sorrow to endure. The first winter that he spent in the White House his two little boys, Willie and Tad, one ten years old and the other eight, fell ill, and Willie's condition became critical.   Daily the President, leaving his office, spent all the time he could at the bedside of the sick child, and at night he often took the nurse's place.   When the end came the father was almost heart-broken, and his grief was well-nigh unbearable.   "My poor

Tad Lincoln.

boy," he murmured, as he stood by the bedside of the dead child, shedding bitter tears. "He was too good for this earth. God has called him home. I know he is much better off in heaven, but we loved him so. It is hard, hard, to have him die."

Willie Lincoln.

But the loss of Willie seemed to make the father cherish more tenderly the little fellow who was left. Tad was with his father much of the time, never hesitating to break in upon him even in the midst of the gravest labors or the most important conferences, sometimes slipping into his father's lap or perching on his shoulder. It is said that at the end of every day Tad came into his father's office, climbed into his father's lap, and told the story of what he had seen and done since early morning. As a rule, he kept on with his childish prattle until he finally fell asleep in his father's arms. Then the President would gently lay him down near his chair and go on with his work. When he had finished he would gather up the sleeping child in his arms and carry him off to bed.

This gives but a glimpse of the tender love that Lincoln had for children, not only his own but all others. It is said that on one occasion, when there was a reception in the White House, three little girls, poorly clad, followed the crowd as they entered the Executive Mansion. Strolling through the building with childish curiosity, they came into the great reception-room, where the people were greeting the President. They were hurrying through in some confusion when Lincoln observed them. "Aren't you going to shake hands with me, little girls?" he said. Then, to the surprise of all who were present and to the great delight of the little girls, he stooped over and warmly shook hands with each.

Another incident is told which reveals Lincoln's love for children. While on the way to Gettysburg, just before making the Gettysburg address, at one of the railroad stations a beautiful little girl handed him through the open window of his car a bunch of rosebuds. As she did so she lisped: "Flowerth for the Prethident." Mr. Lincoln, taking the rosebuds, and bending over to kiss the child, said gently: "You are a sweet rosebud yourself! I hope you will open into perpetual beauty and goodness!"

In such simple, human ways did the lonely man in the White House find a solace for his sorrows and give expression to that which was finest and noblest in his nature.

CHAPTER IX

LINCOLN AND THE EMANCIPATION PROCLAMATION

As you will recall, in his inaugural address on March 4, 1861, it was not slavery that President Lincoln emphasized but the preservation of the Union. This continued to be his chief aim. He believed that upon that great issue he could keep the people of the Northern States united. He also knew that in the border States, Maryland, Kentucky, and Missouri, there were many pro-slavery men who were also pro-Union men, and it was a matter of the first importance to prevent these States from joining the ranks of secession. "These all against us," he said, "and the job on our hands is too large for us. We would as well consent to separation at once, including the surrender of the capital." He felt sure that, if he should interfere with slavery within their borders, they would be likely to go out of the Union.

But with this cautious policy all his subordinates did not agree, and two of his generals took matters into their own hands. On August 30, 1861, General Fremont, who held command in the Western Department, declared martial law there, and at the same time stated that the slaves of men who were fighting against the Union were free men. This was going quite beyond his rightful authority, and Lincoln, refusing to approve the order, declared it void.

He believed that to take such a step would turn the balance in the wavering border States in favor of secession.   In the following May another commander, General Hunter, declared the slaves free in South Carolina, Georgia, and Florida.   Again Lincoln refused to approve, and the order was made void.

In refusing to sanction the drastic actions of Fremont and Hunter, the President met with bitter criticism from many radical anti-slavery men.   They mercilessly censured him.   They insisted that he was too cautious; that his policy was lame and halting; that he himself was not a bold and heroic executive, such as the momentous issues of the hour demanded.

But Lincoln, though sensitive to such criticisms, did not waver.   The plan which he began to lay before the people, before the war had been going on for a year, was gradual emancipation of the slaves, compensation of the owners, and colonization of the negroes after they had received their freedom.   If any State should agree to this plan, Congress was to vote the money to make good to the slave-owners the loss of their property, and in the course of a term of years the slaves in any State agreeing to the plan would be made free.   Such a measure the President believed would be fair to all.   Should the border States fall in with it, they would be putting themselves cordially on the side of the North to preserve the Union.   As it was, they were acrimoniously divided, with the majority probably favoring secession, and only sheer military force held them in the Union.

This plan was urged upon Congress by Lincoln in a special message early in March, 1862; and he made a strong appeal for it to the senators and representatives from the border States especially. But these opposed it so bitterly that the rest of Congress would not take it up.

During all these months, although Lincoln hated slavery as strongly as ever, and although he knew it was at the root of the secession trouble, he held to the view set forth in his inaugural address that even Congress had no constitutional right to interfere with slavery in any States where it already existed. And as for himself, no act of his upon it would have had the slightest legal weight, except as a war necessity accepted by Congress.

In the meantime, however, the anti-slavery feeling was growing in the North. This fact was made evident by two laws that were passed in 1862. One, enacted in April, provided for the emancipation of slaves in the District of Columbia, with payment of a moderate compensation to the owners; the other, passed in June, was an act to secure the freedom of all persons within the Territories.

The war was still growing in intensity, and the Union forces, especially in the East, were making but little headway. Four days after the battle of Bull Run General George B. McClellan had been put at the head of all the Union armies under the President, who was commander-in-

Lincoln at General McClellan's Headquarters.

chief, and had been placed in command of the Army of the Potomac, which was intended for the defense of Washington and the capture of Richmond. General McClellan was only thirty-four years old, but he had had excellent training, at West Point and in the Crimean War, for his responsible position, and had won distinction by a successful campaign in West Virginia. He had the full confidence of the President, who was desirous of co-operating in every possible way. By the opening of the spring campaign in 1862, McClellan had, by thorough organization and drill, created a splendid army.

But the people of the North were not satisfied. They had long been impatient for action and were clamoring for McClellan to push on to Richmond. It was not merely to shorten the time of burdens and losses, but because every week's delay convinced the European nations more and more that the North could never conquer the South, and that to save business and civilization alike they must intervene. Even a year later, just before Gettysburg, a great English writer published a history to come down to "the disruption of the United States."

President Lincoln himself was quite as impatient as anybody. Although McClellan knew all this, he still held the Union army in camp. Day after day the people read in the newspapers: "All is quiet on the Potomac," and they wondered why no move was made. To those who understood just what was going on in Washington, it was clear that the President and the general could not agree as to what should be done. Conference followed conference. Lincoln went to headquarters, and McClellan was called to Cabinet meetings.

The actual reason why McClellan delayed his advance was twofold. In the first place, he had no faith in his half-trained army's fighting power, feared more Bull Runs, and was resolved not to give battle till sure of success; as was said later, he wished to "organize victory." In the second place, he always enormously overestimated the Confederate forces against him, and listened too credulously to every frightened or traitorous story of their great armies.

Moreover, he believed himself the one capable officer of the country, and not only thought but said and wrote that the salvation of the country depended on him alone. He would take suggestions from nobody, even his military superior; much more did he assume that those of civilians were simply worthless. "I was obliged to attend a Cabinet meeting," he wrote to his wife, "and was bored and annoyed. There are some of the greatest geese in the Cabinet I have ever seen—enough to tax the patience of Job."

It was not long before he began to show gross disrespect to the President himself. At times he kept Mr. Lincoln waiting in the anteroom of his house while he attended to business matters with others. Lincoln was not slow to observe these discourtesies, but he overlooked the

outrageous treatment rather than risk impairing McClellan's zeal or influence by a quarrel. With that utter absence of self-pride and devotion to duty which were large elements of his greatness and usefulness, he said: "I will hold McClellan's horse if he will only bring us success."

Lincoln recommended that an advance be made on Richmond overland from the north, in order to keep the Union army between the Confederates and Washington. McClellan objected, knowing there were many rivers to be crossed, every one of which could, for defensive purposes, be made a Confederate stronghold. At last Lincoln consented that McClellan might approach Richmond by way of the peninsula between the James and the York Rivers, but on the express condition that enough troops should be left behind to prevent the national capital from falling into the hands of the Confederates. In this he was not interfering in military matters, but taking only necessary political precautions. For the country demanded such protection; and Confederate possession of Washington even for a week would have been an excuse for European nations at once to recognize the Confederacy and end the war.

No sooner had McClellan gone South than the President's war council induced him to withdraw McDowell's corps of forty thousand men to protect Washington, on the ground that McClellan had not kept his agreement. As McClellan relied on this corps to flank the Confederate army in Virginia and leave his march on Richmond un-

Allan Pinkerton.
President Lincoln.
General McClernand.

On the Battle-Field of Antietam.
From a photograph by Brady.

169

opposed, he regarded this as ruining his campaign, and never ceased to declare later that it did so.

Having reached Fortress Monroe by water, McClellan started from there early in April, 1862, and advanced up the peninsula to Yorktown, to which he laid siege, instead of attempting to capture it by assault at once. This delayed the army an entire month and was needless, for the opposing force was not a third the size of his own. But even after that serious loss of time it took him nearly two months to get within ten miles of Richmond. He kept constantly protesting that his army was too small for him to do what was expected of him, and that he was not receiving from the administration the proper support.

But at last, by the end of May, he was within striking distance of Richmond, waiting for the arrival of McDowell and his army, now promised him once more and marching south from Fredericksburg, not far off. But when one division had reached him, the rest of the corps was ordered back to guard Washington again; for in order to prevent this junction, "Stonewall" Jackson had swept down the Shenandoah Valley, then called the "back door to Washington," and was thought to threaten the city.

McClellan was bitterly disappointed, especially since he had halted his advance to wait for the new troops. He was within five miles of Richmond, and could see its church spires. His forces were still far in excess of the Confederates, who in fact had prepared to evacuate the city.

But believing that the Confederate army was twice as large as his own, he let them attack him first. The result was that he had to retreat and change his base of supplies to the James River.

In deep depression he telegraphed during his retreat to Secretary Stanton at Washington: "I know that a few thousand more men would have changed this battle from a defeat to a victory. As it is, the government must not and cannot hold me responsible for the result. I feel too earnestly to-night. I have seen too many dead and wounded comrades to feel otherwise than that the government has not sustained this army. If you do not do so now, the game is lost. If I save this army now, I tell you plainly that I owe no thanks to you or to any persons in Washington. You have done your best to sacrifice this army."

"Save your army at all events," Lincoln replied, with remarkable tolerance and self-restraint. " . . . I feel any misfortune to you and your army quite as keenly as you feel it yourself. If you have had a drawn battle, or a repulse, it is the price we pay for the enemy not being in Washington. We protected Washington, and the enemy concentrated on you. Had we stripped Washington, he would have been upon us before the troops could have gotten to you."

Stanton had less control over his temper. He said: "If we gave McClellan a million men, he would sit down in the mud and yell for two." It is believed by some military critics that there were enough men to protect Washington without McDowell's troops, and that by recalling them Lincoln prevented McClellan from attaining the great purpose of his campaign—the capture of Richmond. However that may be, the Peninsular Campaign failed and caused bitter disappointment in the North.

The failure was keenly felt by Lincoln also. In the midst of the gloom and dismay which settled upon the North, he visited McClellan at Harrison's Landing early in July, believing that he could in this way get more accurate information of the actual conditions than was possible from McClellan's letters and reports. When Lincoln clearly saw the true military situation, he made up his mind that some drastic measure should be adopted to strengthen the Union cause. He was now ready to take definite steps toward emancipating the slaves within the Confederate lines as a war measure. It seemed absolutely necessary in order to save the Union.

It is said that he finally decided upon the Emancipation Proclamation while on the boat, July 8, on his return from his visit to McClellan's headquarters. Four days later he had a conference at the White House with the border State representatives. He earnestly urged them to adopt his policy and accept compensation for their slaves. He reminded them of the hope entertained by States which were in rebellion "that their sister slave communities would join the Confederacy." But, to his keen and even bitter disappointment, his appeal was made in vain, for the majority of them rejected his plan. Of course this did not concern his proclamation, which did not affect loyal States or districts; but it would greatly have aided its moral effect, and joined with it would have freed all the slaves instead of only a part.

He had now done his best to secure compensated emancipation, but had failed. There was only one other course for him to consider. He said to a Southerner, who had begged him not to issue the proclamation, and told him wrongly that he could not legally do it, "What I cannot do of course I will not do, but it may as well be understood once and for all that I shall not surrender this game leaving any available card unemployed. I have about come to the conclusion," he added, "that I must free the slaves by proclamation or we ourselves will be subdued."

On the day following the conference with the border States' representatives, while driving to the funeral of Secretary Stanton's infant son, Lincoln had a talk with Secretaries Seward and Welles about the topic which was making so strong an appeal to him, that is, the emancipation of the slaves. He argued that since the slaves were greatly aiding the Confederate cause, some by producing food to aid the Confederate armies, some by acting as teamsters, and others by doing various forms of labor in Confederate camps, and for other reasons, it would be wise to adopt some measure by which these slaves could help the Union rather than the Confederate cause.

After much anxious thought he called a Cabinet meeting on July 22. In opening the meeting he said he was going to communicate something about which he did not wish them to offer any advice, since his decision had already been reached. He said that he intended no disrespect to any member, but that having finally reached a decision he would stand by it, for he believed it was right. He added that he should be glad to have them offer any suggestions as to details, but nothing more.

Then he read, greatly to the surprise probably of all but Seward and Welles, the first rough draft of an emancipation proclamation which he had in mind to issue. In this he declared it to be his intention to recommend that Congress adopt at its next session some plan of emancipation. He again stated the purpose of the war as being the preservation of the Union; and, "as a fit and necessary military measure for effecting this object," he declared that "on January 1, 1863, all slaves in States wherein the constitutional authority of the United States was not recognized should be thenceforward and forever free."

After a few slight verbal changes had been made in the proclamation, Seward offered the only important suggestion of the meeting. He urged delay. "I suggest," he said, "that you postpone its issue until you can give it to the country supported by military success instead of issuing it, as would be the case now, upon the greatest disaster of the war." Then he added his fear that it would be considered "the last shriek on the retreat."

Lincoln and the Cabinet approved this suggestion. Then the meeting adjourned, with the understanding

The First Reading of the Emancipation Proclamation.
From the painting by F. B. *Carpenter.*

that, for the present, all should strictly keep the secret of the President's purpose; and Lincoln put the proclamation aside to await the Union victory for which he longed.

In the meantime criticism and abuse were heaped upon Lincoln by both slavery and anti-slavery men from all parts of the country. On one occasion, after listening patiently to a group of callers who had come to him with complaints of his failures, Lincoln said to them:

"Gentlemen, suppose all the property you were worth were in gold and you had put it in the hands of Blondin [the most famous of tight-rope walkers], to carry across the Niagara River on a rope. Would you shake the cable or keep shouting at him: 'Blondin, stand up a little straighter. Blondin, stoop a little more—go a little faster—lean a little more to the north—lean a little more to the south'? No, you would hold your breath, as well as your tongue, and keep your hands off until he was safe over. The government is carrying an enormous weight, untold treasures are in their hands; they are doing the very best they can. Don't badger them. Keep silence and we will take you safe across."

Among Lincoln's critics were many influential men who were continually urging him to take some definite action in the direction of emancipating the slaves. The bitter abuse by the press reached its culminating point in a signed editorial written by Horace Greeley for the New York *Tribune* August 19, 1862, with the heading "The Prayer of Twenty Millions." This was a criticism of Lincoln for his failure to adopt some definite plan of emancipating the slaves.

Three days later Abraham Lincoln answered this editorial in a public letter which was printed in the columns of the *National Intelligencer*, a newspaper which was published in Washington. In this letter Lincoln said: "My paramount object in this struggle is to save the Union, and is not to save or destroy slavery. If I could save the Union without freeing any slave, I would do it; and if I could save it by freeing some and leaving others alone, I would also do that. What I do about slavery and the colored race, I do because I believe it helps to save the Union, and what I forbear to do, I forbear because I do not believe it would help to save the Union."

This letter was a singularly shrewd political move. It held back from opposition great numbers, who thought the country had no right to abolish slavery, and many more who thought it had no interest in doing so. But beyond this it was a remarkable state paper. It was remarkable for its clearness, its simplicity, and its strength, as well as for its manly courage. It made a deep impression upon the country, and especially upon the plain people, who were strongly in sympathy with Lincoln. They admired and loved him. They believed that he was honest, and trusted him because they thought they understood him, and they felt that he understood them.

There was good reason for this strong bond of good feeling between Lincoln and the people, for during all his administration he was ever ready to take the people into his confidence. If in any part of the country some criticism by factional leaders sprang up as to what he was doing or not doing, it was his habit to appeal to the people by writing such a letter as the one we have just discussed. These letters, brushing aside matters of minor importance, always seized upon the main issue. They were always written in simple, sincere English that the people could understand; and they put arguments into the mouths of Lincoln's admirers and followers which had a wonderful effect in strengthening public sentiment in his favor. These letters were effective instruments in his masterful leadership.

During the whole summer of 1862 Lincoln's critics were severe upon him for his failure to set the slaves free. Their clamor increased, and deputations and committees in great numbers waited upon him. He was censured in the press, in the pulpit, and on the platform. One of the deputations, made up of clergymen from various religious denominations in Chicago, came to him on September 13, and requested that he issue at once a proclamation of universal emancipation. After arguing with them, to draw out their full and free expression of opinion, Lincoln replied: "I have not decided against a proclamation of liberty to the slaves, but hold the matter under advisement, and I assure you that the subject is on my mind by day and night more than any other. Whatever shall appear to be God's will I will do. I trust that the freedom with which I have canvassed your views has not in any respect injured your feelings."

When they indicated that he was not carrying out the will of the people, and that the will of the people was also the divine will on this matter of emancipation, he replied: "I hope it will not be irreverent for me to say that if it is probable that God would reveal his will to others on a

Lincoln Receiving the Delegation of Clergymen from Chicago.

point so connected with my duty, it might be supposed he would reveal it directly to me; for, unless I am more deceived in myself than I often am, it is my earnest desire to know the will of Providence in this matter, and if I can learn what it is I will do it."

Lincoln's power to keep his own counsel is shown by the fact that at the very time when abusive editorials were being published, and when these Chicago clergymen were strongly urging him to emancipate the slaves, the first draft of his Emancipation Proclamation was already written and lying in his desk. But no one knew anything about it except the members of his Cabinet, who had kept the secret well. Committees and individuals continued to come and discuss the question of the freeing of the slaves with Lincoln, and almost always he argued the matter as if he were opposed to it. In this way he was balancing the question and weighing the sentiment of the people, in order to make sure that he was reaching a right conclusion.

And so the summer wore away. It was on September 17 that the victory came for which Lincoln was waiting. On that day the battle of Antietam, won by Union forces, drove Lee out of Maryland. Five days later Lincoln called together his Cabinet. After some general conversation he took up a book which the humorist Artemus Ward, its author, had just sent to him. From this book he read two chapters which he thought were very funny. He laughed heartily, but not a member of the Cabinet smiled. Throwing his book down, he heaved a long sigh and said: "Gentlemen, why don't you laugh? With the fearful strain that is upon me night and day, if I did not laugh I should die, and you need this medicine as much as I do."

Then, changing to a serious tone of voice, he drew forth from his tall hat a paper and spoke as follows:

"The rebel army is now driven out of Maryland, and I am going to fulfil the promise I made to myself and"— hesitating—"to my Maker. I have gotten you together to hear what I have written down; I do not wish your ad-

Burnside Bridge, Antietam.

vice about the main thing, for that I have determined for myself." Then followed his reading of the proclamation for freedom, the pith of which is contained in the following sentence:

"On the first day of January in the year of our Lord one thousand eight hundred and sixty-three, all persons held as slaves within any State or designated part of a State, the people whereof shall then be in rebellion against the United States, shall be then, thenceforth, and forever free."

...statesmen were silent. The tremendous importance of the words they had heard broke upon them. The man whom they had thought lacking in seriousness sat before them in grim determination, about to send forth an edict that would profoundly affect the destiny of the nation.

Then Secretary Stanton said: "Mr. President, if the reading of Artemus Ward is the prelude to such a deed as this the author should be canonized." And all said: "Amen."

In the long and bitter struggle through which Lincoln had passed in reaching a decision to issue the Emancipation Proclamation, he had asked himself many searching questions: "Will not the act be that of a dictator? Will it not do more harm than good? Will it not injure the loyal men of the South?" According to his own account, he had prayed to the Almighty to save him from the necessity of issuing the proclamation, and, in the language of Gethsemane, he had

General Robert E. Lee.

The statesmen were silent. The tremendous importance of the words they had heard broke upon them. The man whom they had thought lacking in seriousness sat before them in grim determination, about to send forth an edict that would profoundly affect the destiny of the nation.

General Robert E. Lee.

Then Secretary Stanton said: "Mr. President, if the reading of Artemus Ward is the prelude to such a deed as this, the author should be canonized." And all said: "Amen."

In the long and bitter struggle through which Lincoln had passed in reaching a decision to issue the Emancipation Proclamation, he had asked himself many searching questions: "Will not the act be that of a dictator? Will it not do more harm than good? Will it not injure the loyal men of the South?" According to his own account, he had prayed to the Almighty to save him from the necessity of issuing the proclamation, and, in the language of Gethsemane, he had

said: "If it be possible, let this cup pass from me."
Even on the day after the fateful step had been taken
he said: "I can only trust in God that I have made no
mistake."

In spite of the clamor that had been raised in some sections to force such a measure, the announcement of the
Emancipation Proclamation, given to the country on September 22, was a surprise to the people, and its immediate
results were by no means reassuring. Although many
newspapers and prominent men commended the Emancipation Proclamation, the country did not accept it with any
signs of special satisfaction. The distrust of Lincoln among
his critics was as great as ever. Many leading politicians
believed the country was moving toward destruction. In
five great States, among them Lincoln's own State of Illinois, the majorities in the autumn elections went against
his party, and the number of men enlisting for service in
the army dropped off very considerably. The signs of dis-
favor were so great that many people wondered whether
Lincoln would issue the Emancipation Proclamation at the
time announced, January 1, 1863.

When Congress met, early in December (1862), he once
more made a strong appeal to that body for his favorite
plan of compensated emancipation; to include the States
in rebellion also, and so induce them to make peace and
remove the great wrong of slavery from the Union. But
the appeal was vain. So on December 30 he called his

Cabinet together and read the document as he had modified it, asking for their criticisms and suggestions. The next day at the Cabinet meeting each member handed these in writing to Mr. Lincoln. He took them all to his office and rewrote the document during the afternoon and next morning. Leaving it to be engrossed, he went at eleven o'clock to the New Year's reception, which kept him until about the middle of the afternoon. Then he went back to the office, where he found the Emancipation Proclamation ready, awaiting his signature.

Frederick Seward writes:

"The broad sheet was spread before him on the Cabinet table. Mr. Lincoln dipped his pen in the ink and then holding it a moment above the paper seemed to hesitate. Looking around, he said: 'I never in my life felt more certain that I was doing right than I do in signing this paper. But I have been shaking hands since nine (eleven?) o'clock this morning, till my arm is stiff and numb. Now this signature is one that will be closely examined, and if they find that my hand trembled, they will say: "He had some compunction." But anyway it is going to be done.'"

So saying, he slowly and carefully wrote at the bottom of the Proclamation: "Abraham Lincoln." A simple act, but one which ultimately struck the shackles from three million human beings and undermined an institution almost as old as the human race.

It must, of course, be remembered that this measure

did not immediately emancipate any slaves whatever. Had it professed to do so, it would have been mere waste paper; for Lincoln had no more power to act contrary to the Constitution than any private citizen. But as commander of the national armies, he had power to take any action needed to weaken the enemy. Hence the document emancipated not the slaves in the loyal border States, nor even in Confederate districts already conquered, but only in those *to be* conquered and when they should be conquered. Its effect was all in the future, and that kept increasing as more and more territory was brought under Union sway. Nearly a million slaves were still left to be emancipated by the Thirteenth Amendment after the war; but even those largely owed their freedom to the earlier measure.

Even at this time Lincoln did not feel certain whether the Emancipation Proclamation would bring gain or loss to the Union cause. He thought it would bring gain, and having come to this decision, he was willing to take the risk.

We might suppose that his anti-slavery critics would now have given him due credit for his courage. But not so. Even this heroic action seemed, for a time, to divide the North. The extreme abolitionists were angry that it did not wipe out slavery altogether, though it could not; the extreme Democrats, of course, thought it a social and political wrong; while great numbers of moderate people were dismayed because it put an end to their favorite plan of winning back the South by conciliation. As to the South, their fury was unmeasured. "The greatest political crime and the greatest political blunder of modern times," one newspaper called it.

But there were two other results which amply justified Lincoln. The greatest was a much more favorable attitude in the best countries of Europe toward the North. Its most important effect in this way was definitely to align on the Union side the weight of England, which as the champion of human freedom never again seriously considered interfering for the Confederacy. The second was the enlisting of scores of thousands of black men as soldiers in the Union army. As the North brought under control more and more of the area of secession, the slaves in increasing numbers joined the Union armies and thus greatly strengthened the chances of success for the Union cause.

All told, more than one hundred and eighty-six thousand negroes took up arms on the side of the Union. This transfer of negro men from Southern plantations to the armies which were striving to conquer the South had a twofold effect. It weakened the South by reducing the number of men who were working to feed and support the Confederate armies, and by just so much did it add strength to the Union armies. The prejudice in the North against the use of the blacks as soldiers rapidly passed away. These men fought bravely, and in so doing not only helped to save the Union, but also to make it clear that the issue of the Emancipation Proclamation was an act of true statesmanship.

CHAPTER · X

THE DARKEST PERIOD OF THE WAR

In spite of the advantages that came from freeing the slaves, the military situation was still far from satisfactory. After the failure of the Peninsular Campaign, McClellan was ordered to return to Washington with his army. His withdrawal relieved the Confederate capital, and Lee, marching swiftly northward, defeated the Union army under General Pope near Washington in the second battle of Bull Run. This defeat caused almost as great a panic in Washington as the first battle of Bull Run, and general discouragement to the defenders of the Union. McClellan's hostile critics—and their number was large—blamed him because he had not been prompt in sending his troops to Pope's support. Lincoln himself said to one of his secretaries: "McClellan has acted badly toward Pope. He really wanted him to fail."

A wave of hot indignation spread over the country, and the Cabinet sent a signed protest to the President against keeping McClellan longer in command of any army of the United States.

But, although in the field he had sorely disappointed the administration as well as the loyal people of the North, he had shown remarkable power in organizing the splendid

Lincoln in 1863.
From a photograph by Brady.

Army of the Potomac and was very popular with his men. Both the officers and the soldiers had confidence in him and loved him. So, even in the face of strenuous opposition, Lincoln, in his great necessity, appointed him once more in command of the troops around Washington. It was a time of crisis and, as usual, Lincoln did his own thinking.

He depended upon McClellan quickly to put the troops into form after their defeat, and to follow sharply after Lee, who was headed for Maryland. This time McClellan did not disappoint the President. He overtook Lee at Antietam, where, as we have noted, he defeated him on September 17, 1862. Lincoln expected McClellan to follow up his victory closely and attack the Confederates before they could get away; but, apparently satisfied with the beginning of success, he settled back into his old tactics of cautious waiting. He allowed Lee to escape across the Potomac River, and, in spite of Lincoln's repeated urging, refused to follow. He said that the troops could not do it for lack of supplies, and that should they try, they would risk severe defeat.

After about three weeks Lincoln went in person to McClellan's camp, where he reviewed the army, talked with the generals, and carefully studied the situation. Then so certain was he of the ability of the army to win a victory that on the next day after his return to Washington he sent McClellan the following order: "The President directs that you cross the Potomac and give battle to the enemy or drive him south." But the obstinate general, alleging, among other things, that the cavalry horses had sore mouths, still remained inactive.

Grievously tried and disappointed over McClellan's persistent failure to force Lee's army to another battle, about November first Lincoln removed him from command and put Burnside in his place. Burnside, one of McClellan's officers and his intimate friend, was a handsome and brave man, with nothing of that self-confidence that was so marked a trait in McClellan. So modest indeed was he that he had twice refused the command of the Army of the Potomac be-

General Ambrose E. Burnside.

cause, to use his own words, he was "not competent to handle so large an army." But there were few for Lincoln to choose from and, unfortunately for himself and for the brave men under him, Burnside accepted the weighty responsibility.

The new commander followed Lee int Virginia and
took up a position facing him at Fredericksburg. Burnside was not ready to give battle until about the middle
of December. Then he ...... a rash assault upon Lee's
troops strongly fortified the heights of Fredericks-

Shattered homes after the battle

...... was repulsed. His losses were so heavy that the
army had to withdraw.

...... the battle Burnside admitted that he alone
...... the failure and declared that his army
...... the highest praise. The disaster had been
...... had the confidence of his army and the
...... the President in grief and anxiety again had
......

The new commander followed Lee into Virginia and took up a position facing him at Fredericksburg. Burnside was not ready to give battle until about the middle of December. Then he made a rash assault upon Lee's troops, strongly fortified upon the heights of Fredericks-

Fredericksburg, Showing Ruins after the Battle.

burg, and was defeated. His losses were so heavy that the Union army had to withdraw.

In reporting the battle Burnside admitted that he alone was responsible for the failure and declared that his army was worthy of the highest praise. The disaster had been so great that he lost the confidence of his army and the country, and the President, in grief and anxiety, again had to look for a general.

Among the officers who had severely criticised the leadership of General Burnside was General Hooker. His soldiers liked to call him "Fighting Joe"—a nickname that indicated his popularity with the men in the ranks—for he was dashing and fearless. But whether he was big enough to manage and direct the Army of the Potomac when pitted against an able general like Lee, no one could tell. The President was just as uncertain as anybody. It was a depressing outlook. Yet Lincoln had to make the decision, and knowing no better man, he appointed Hooker, having faith in his ability and patriotism and in the high esteem in which his soldiers held him. To put the new general on his guard, however, he wrote him a letter, in which he frankly but gently admonished him. Here is the letter, which clearly indicates the President's self-control at this time of trial:

"I have placed you at the head of the Army of the Potomac. Of course I have done this upon what appeared to me to be sufficient reasons, and yet I think it best for you to know that there are some things in regard to which I am not quite satisfied with you. . . . I have heard, in such a way as to believe it, of your recently saying that both the army and the government needed a dictator. . . . Only those generals who gain successes can set up as dictators. What I now ask of you is military success, and I will risk the dictatorship. The government will support you to the utmost of its ability, which is neither more nor less than it has done and will do for all commanders. I much fear that the spirit which you have aided to infuse

into the army, of criticising their commander and with-
holding confidence from him, will now turn upon you. I
will assist you as far as I can to put it down. Neither you
nor Napoleon, if he were alive again, could get any good
out of any army while such a spirit prevails in it; and now,

General Joseph Hooker.

beware of rashness! Beware of rashness; but, with energy and sleepless vigilance, go forward and give us victories."

When Hooker had finished reading the letter, he was
so affected by its kindly spirit that tears came to his eyes.
Folding it and putting it into his pocket, he remarked:
"That is just such a letter as a father might write his son.
It is a beautiful letter and, although I think he is harder

on me than I deserve, I will say that I love the man who wrote it."

Having appointed Hooker, the President felt that he must support and assist him to the best of his ability. So on April 4 he visited Hooker's headquarters. Again he wished to find out for himself the true situation. He found that the army had been put into splendid form, but still he had gloomy forebodings. When he reached the camp and reviewed the long lines of "Boys in Blue," there was no joy in his face. Sadness was there—the sadness of some threatening calamity. One of the soldiers who looked into Abraham Lincoln's face that day wrote afterward as follows:

"None of us to our dying day can forget that countenance! From its presence we marched directly onward toward our camp, and as soon as 'Route step!' was ordered and the men were free to talk, they spoke thus to each other: 'Did you ever see such a look on any man's face?' 'He is bearing the burden of the nation.' 'It is an awful load. It is killing him.' 'Yes, that is so; he is not long for this world.' Concentrated in that one great, strong, yet tender face, the agony of the life-or-death struggle was revealed as we had never seen it before. With new understanding we knew why we were soldiers."

And Lincoln's forebodings proved truly prophetic; for the next battle, fought at Chancellorsville on May 1, 2, 3, and 4, was another awful slaughter of the Union army, another case of brave men fighting under incompetent leadership. From thousands of mourning homes throughout the North letters had already come, urging the folly and cruelty of sending brave men into battle under weak generals. Now a fresh flood of despair poured itself through the same channel into the White House, meeting the rush of disastrous news from the battlefield. The President's heart was torn with grief. The terrible strain under which he labored would have broken down a man of less physical and mental vigor.

Noah Brooks, who was then in Washington as a newspaper correspondent, gives a vivid account of the bitter sorrow and suffering which the news of this defeat brought to Lincoln:

"About three o'clock in the afternoon," he writes, "the door opened and Lincoln came into the room. I shall never forget that picture of despair. He held a telegram in his hand. He gave me the telegram, and in a voice trembling with emotion said: 'Read it.' Never as long as I knew him did he seem to be so broken up, so dispirited, so ghost-like. Clasping his hands behind his back, he walked up and down the room, saying: 'My God! My God! What will the country say? What will the country say?'"

That night was an agonizing one for Lincoln. His secretary, working across the hall, heard the tread of the President's footsteps, back and forth, back and forth, till, at three o'clock, his own work finished, he went home.

When he returned at eight, he found the President in his office, calm and hopeful, drinking his coffee, which had been sent in. On his desk lay a letter of instructions to General Hooker. It expressed no lack of confidence, but gave orders to push forward and fight again. During the long hours in which Lincoln had wrestled with the forces of despair, he had worked out a plan to meet the trying situation, and had come to the firm determination to push the war with all the resources at his command.

This matter of finding generals was one of Lincoln's most perplexing problems. When the Southern States seceded, many of the best-known generals went with them; and it took time for the Union armies to develop and reveal leadership. It was a unique situation for the President. Almost without military training or experience, he was called upon to plan and direct military movements, because as yet no one had been found in the army capable of assuming that responsibility. After McClellan's failure before Richmond, the President had felt that he must have a man of military training to advise him, and had appointed General Halleck; but in the crisis that followed the Union defeat at the second battle of Bull Run Halleck had left the President to decide, and was therefore of little avail.

Perhaps it was fortunate that the decisions rested upon Lincoln; for history has confirmed the military plans of the President, as revealed in his notes, to have been sound. It is known that he applied himself to the study of military science and to the geography of campaigns with the same systematic care that he would have given to a law case. Above all, his common sense and good judgment carried him through many critical situations. Then, too, however dark and threatening the outlook, he never lost courage nor faith in final victory.

There was need of all these strong qualities in the winter of 1862 and the spring of 1863, for it was the darkest period of the war. The people in the North were angry and unhappy. The war had cost many thousands of brave young lives; and aside from this human toll, it was costing the country two million dollars a day. Yet there was almost nothing to show for it in the way of success on the battle-field. Countless letters of protest against this terrible waste were heaped upon Lincoln's desk. But how was Lincoln to turn defeat into victory? He had a fine army, brave, loyal, and disciplined. If only he could find the right general!

CHAPTER XI

GETTYSBURG AND THE TURNING OF THE TIDE

ABOUT a month later, while the Army of the Potomac was still holding its position opposite Lee's army on the Rappahannock, Lee quietly left his quarters and started on his second invasion of the North. Hooker followed him skilfully until they had both crossed the Potomac, and then, quarrelling with Halleck, he resigned. It was but another incident of petty bickering and jealousy which in those trying days embarrassed the Union cause and hindered the President in his conduct of the war. General Meade, another corps officer, was appointed to succeed Hooker.

Great was the people's consternation at this sudden change of generals on the eve of a great battle. Washington was under a terrible strain, and the North, panic-stricken, stood appalled. What must have been the feelings of Lincoln as he awaited the outcome of the battle that was to decide the fate of the nation!

The new commander, with desperate energy, pressed so closely upon the heels of Lee that the latter had to turn, at Gettysburg, Pennsylvania, and attack him. There during three hot summer days (July 1, 2, 3) the two armies fought one of the great battles of the world. On the last day, from one o'clock in the afternoon to three, General

Lee kept up a continuous cannonade upon the Union centre, following it with a great infantry attack. The charge failed, General Lee, with his veterans of Fredericksburg and Chancellorsville, suffered defeat, and the Union cause was safe. On the 4th of July the frightened North learned, with a sigh of relief, that the Confederate army had begun to retreat toward the Potomac.

General George Gordon Meade.

The President was strongly urging Meade to pursue and engage Lee's shattered army in another battle before it could cross the Potomac. Meade did follow closely, but not knowing how badly shattered Lee's army was, and believing the situation too critical to risk an attack upon the strongly fortified Confederate army on the heights in front of the Potomac, he allowed him to escape unhindered. Like McClellan after Antietam, he would not take the chance of a second battle, although by so doing he might, as many thought, have crushed, or perhaps even captured Lee's army, and have brought the war to a close with victory for the Union.

Lincoln, believing this, was so distressed that he paced the floor in deathly pallor, wringing his hands in agony. His anxiety so wrought upon him that he could not shake it off. Twelve days after the battle, he sent these bitter words in a telegram to Simon Cameron, his former Secretary of War: "I would give much to be relieved of the impression that Meade, Couch, Smith, and all, since the battle of Gettysburg, have striven only to get Lee over the river without another fight."

On the preceding day he had written a letter to General Meade, expressing his sorrow and dissatisfaction.

". . . My dear General," he said, "I do not believe you appreciate the magnitude of the misfortune involved in Lee's escape. He was within your easy grasp, and to have closed upon him would, in connection with our other late successes, have ended the war. As it is, the war will be prolonged indefinitely. It would be unreasonable to expect, and I do not expect, that you can now effect much. Your golden opportunity is gone. I am distressed immeasurably because of it. I beg you will not consider this a prosecution or persecution of yourself. As you have learned that I was dissatisfied, I have thought it best to kindly tell you why."

But after thinking it over, he did not send the letter,

because the Confederate army had already escaped, and he did not wish to dishearten General Meade for the task still before him.

A saving feature of the general situation relieved the terrible gloom cast upon Lincoln by Meade's failure to put in the finishing stroke. On the same day that Lee began his retreat, July 4, 1863, General Grant received the surrender of Vicksburg, with thirty-two thousand men. Four days later Port Hudson also fell into the hands of the Union forces. This was the last Confederate stronghold on the Mississippi River, which was now entirely under the control of the Union. As the Mississippi was second only in importance to the Potomac, its control by the Union could not but cheer the President and lighten the depression of the White House.

These victories marked the turning of the tide in favor of the Union. Lee had hoped to win a great victory on Northern soil. He had hoped to capture the city of Philadelphia, perhaps Baltimore and Washington, and thus strike a blow severe enough to bring the war to a close. But from this time the Confederate cause was doomed, although it was not so clear then as it is now.

The little town of Gettysburg had thus been the field of one of the decisive battles of the world. There had fallen six thousand six hundred "Boys in Blue" and "Boys in Gray," and there they were buried on Cemetery Ridge. This spot, made sacred by the sacrifice of so many lives, was set apart as a national cemetery. November 19, the day appointed for its consecration, a vast company assembled to do honor to the occasion. The heat of summer had passed, and the leaves of autumn lay scattered over the graves of the heroes who had here given up their lives.

Gettysburg in War Time.

Edward Everett was to deliver the oration. President Lincoln was invited to be present and to say a few words in accepting and setting apart this spot to its sacred use. Everett's able and eloquent address, lasting two hours, was listened to with rapt attention by the throng of one hundred thousand people.

When Mr. Lincoln arose and came forward, the vast

audience, which had been unable to see him where he sat on the platform, looked with curious interest upon his towering figure. For a moment he stood with bowed head and hands clasped behind him. So impressed were the people with the sad-eyed countenance, furrowed with heavy care and sorrow, that they almost forgot to cheer. For a moment he met their gaze in silence as if unconscious of their presence, and then began to speak in his high treble voice as follows:

"Four score and seven years ago our fathers brought forth upon this continent a new nation, conceived in liberty, and dedicated to the proposition that all men are created equal. Now we are engaged in a great civil war, testing whether that nation, or any nation so conceived and so dedicated, can long endure. We are met on a great battlefield of that war. We have come to dedicate a portion of that field as a final resting-place for those who here gave their lives that that nation might live. It is altogether fitting and proper that we should do this. But in a larger sense we cannot dedicate, we cannot consecrate, we cannot hallow this ground. The brave men, living and dead, who struggled here, have consecrated it far above our power to add or detract. The world will little note, nor long remember, what we say here, but it can never forget what they did here. It is for us, the living, rather to be dedicated here to the unfinished work which they who fought here have thus far so nobly advanced. It is rather for us to be

Lincoln and Tad.
From a photograph by Brady taken at the White House.

here dedicated to the great task remaining before us, that from these honored dead we take increased devotion to that cause for which they gave the last full measure of devotion; that we here highly resolve that these dead shall not have died in vain; that this nation, under God, shall have a new birth of freedom, and that government of the people, by the people, and for the people, shall not perish from the earth."

Hardly had his hearers settled themselves to listen when he sat down, to the great surprise of all, for he had been speaking only two minutes. It was therefore natural that the applause should not be hearty and enthusiastic. Even the distinguished men on the platform failed to realize that there had been spoken one of the world's masterpieces. Some of his friends and admirers also were greatly disappointed.

"He has made a failure," remarked Everett, "and I am sorry for it. His speech was not equal to him."

Lincoln himself said: "Lamon, that speech won't scour. It is a flat failure. The people are disappointed."

But when men saw the address in printed form, they were struck with its power and beauty. Then they knew that in poetic feeling, purity of language, and nobility of thought, it was a flawless gem. After reading it, Edward Everett wrote to Lincoln: "I should be glad if I could flatter myself that I came as near the central idea of the occasion in two hours as you did in two minutes."

The Gettysburg address fittingly symbolizes the spirit of Abraham Lincoln. In it are revealed the sincerity, sympathy, and tenderness of his nature, and his lofty conception of what should be our nation's sublime purpose and aspiration. It was as if for a brief moment the soul of the man were set free in speech, and then quickly retired to its hiding-place in the rugged human temple where nature had enshrined it.

CHAPTER XII

LINCOLN'S SIMPLICITY AND FRIENDLINESS

TURNING aside for a little from the strenuous anxieties and heavy burdens which made up for the most part the daily life of the President, we are cheered and warmed by many friendly and tender incidents in his experience. They are like sunshine filtering through a darkening forest, not only beautiful in themselves, but throwing beneficent light on their gloomy surroundings. A few will serve to show his kindly attitude toward those in humble walks of life, and his gracious bearing toward those who looked to him for sympathy or help.

But first let us look at Lincoln himself in his most human aspect, apart from the requirements of his office. Into his exalted position as head of the nation, girt round with accepted social conventions, he carried the simplicity of the backwoods life, hardly giving thought to the ordinary formalities of every-day living.

He spent nearly all his time earnestly at work in his office. Even when he went to the dining-room, he was quite as likely as not to sit at the table lost in thought without really knowing what he ate. It was not unusual for him to be so weighed down with care and anxiety as to

Lincoln with His Family.

From the painting by Alonzo Chappel. Copyright by H. B. Hall's Sons.

209

forget to go to his meals at all. Then some food was sent on a tray to his office—a glass of milk, or some crackers and fruit, satisfied him. He was a light eater, and his diet was simple.

His dress was as plain as his food was simple. When at work in his office he generally had on slippers. In summer he often wore a faded linen duster, and in winter, on going out during the day, he frequently wrapped around his shoulders an old gray shawl instead of putting on an overcoat.

He kept up his country habit of rising early, and was often at work by six o'clock. One morning at that hour, a stranger passing the White House saw Mr. Lincoln standing in the gateway, apparently waiting for something. The President remarked: "I am looking for a newsboy. If you see one when you turn the corner, please send him to me."

Although his days were long and crowded with cares, he was never too busy to help those who sought his aid. He would listen with patience to an appeal from any man or woman, even the humblest citizen. One day two women called to beg for the release of two men in jail for resisting the draft. Their request led Lincoln to release all the men in the same jail for that offense. To a friend close by he said: "These fellows have suffered long enough."

The elder of the women, an aged mother, was much affected, and said to the President quietly as she was leaving: "I shall probably never see you again until we meet in Heaven." This touched the President keenly, and his friend, observing the effect, said to him: "You are too sensitive a man and too sympathetic to endure such trying scenes every day. You should protect your nerves and your strength against such an ordeal." "Things of the sort you have just seen don't hurt me," Lincoln replied. "It is the only thing to-day that has made me forget my condition or has given me any pleasure." Then he added these beautiful words: "Die when I may, I wish it said of me by those who know me best that I always plucked a thistle and planted a flower where I thought a flower would grow."

On another occasion—and official burdens were unusually heavy that day—a throng of men and women were waiting in the White House for an opportunity to talk with him, when a friend remarked:

"Mr. President, you had better send that throng away. You are too tired to see any more people this afternoon. Have them sent away, for you will wear yourself out listening to them."

"They don't want much, and they get very little," he replied. "Each one considers his business of great importance, and I must gratify them. I know how I should feel if I were in their place."

In no way did Lincoln's tender, gentle, sympathetic nature find better expression than in his personal relations with the soldiers. Most of them were not more than twenty-one years of age,* many were less; so in their blue capes and caps they were in fact as in name "Boys in Blue."

Lincoln's first visits to the soldier boys were when they were encamped just outside of Washington, before they had had any experience of campaigns and battles, or knew anything of the cruelties and hardships of war. It was there that many came to know him, to feel his friendly hand-clasp, to receive his "God bless you," and to believe that he cared for them not only as soldiers but as men.

When he visited their camp, and passed down the long rows of tents, he showed an interest in everything that touched their daily lives. To their hearty greetings he answered by smiles and nods, and in many ways revealed to them that he was indeed the soldiers' friend. Later in the war, Lincoln visited the soldiers when they were encamped on the Rappahannock River and at Antietam. There, as at Washington in the earlier days, he made it plain to each man that he was a personal friend. "Father Abraham" they loved to call him, and to him every man bearing a musket was a son. Looking upon his sorrow-stricken but kindly face, they said: "He cares for us; he makes us fight, but he cares."

One company that was stationed at the Soldiers' Home just outside of Washington, where Mr. Lincoln had his summer cottage, was especially favored by daily associa-

* Of the 2,500,000 "Boys in Blue" who enlisted during the war, more than 2,000,000 were under 21 years old, more than 1,000,000 were not 18; 800,000 were under 17; 200,000 under 16, and 100,000 under 15.

tion with him. They acted as guard for Mr. Lincoln in his comings and goings between Washington and their camp; and sometimes when they were at mess he would say: "That coffee smells good, boys. Give me a cup," or "How are these beans, boys? Let me have a plate."

Sanitary Commission Lodge, Washington.

The fortunate captain of this company, by request of Mr. Lincoln, took breakfast with him every morning, and then accompanied the President as guard to the White House.

"It was Mr. Lincoln's custom, on account of the pressure of business," said the captain, "to breakfast before the other members of the family were up; and I usually entered his room at six thirty or seven o'clock in the morning, where I

often found him reading the Bible or some work on the
art of war. On my entering he would read aloud and offer
comments of his own on what he read."

Not only did the fresh recruits learn to look for the
President's visits, but the wounded soldiers as well. They

Harewood Hospital near Washington.

were brought to Washington by the thousand, filling the
hospitals to overflowing and crowding the parks and streets
—crippled men with leg or arm missing, and with worn,
haggard faces. To all of these Abraham Lincoln extended
a personal attention that revealed his kindness in countless ways. In the hospitals, as he passed by cot after cot,
he would stop now and then to shake hands or utter cheering words to the sick and the suffering. Thus did his loving
spirit go out to those who stood in need of him.

Oftentimes a flash of Lincoln's humor would bring a quick laugh and brighten the whole day for the sufferers. One day in a crowded hospital it was whispered from cot to cot that Lincoln was in the building and would soon pass by. All who could stand did so, with hands by their sides, ready to salute their commander. A soldier from Pennsylvania, who had been wounded in the shoulder, was one of these. He was a giant in size, six feet seven inches tall—that being three inches taller than the President. When Lincoln approached him, he stopped in amazement. Looking up from the feet to the head and

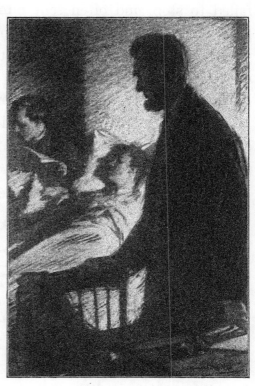

Lincoln·Visiting Wounded Soldiers.

then down from the head to the feet of this tall man, he stood speechless. After a few seconds of silence he grasped the giant by the hand, exclaiming: "Hello, comrade, do you know when your feet get cold?"

A case that was especially touching was that of "Little

Johnnie," who had been in the hospital a long time. He was hopelessly crippled, and beyond recovery. But he was always cheerful and was much liked by all who knew him. In passing the cot of this little sufferer, Lincoln never failed to stop, and often sent him, through Mrs. Lincoln, fruit and flowers, and a friendly message.

But it was especially the youthful soldiers who hād committed some offense against military discipline that he bore upon his heart with a truly paternal solicitude. Here is an example in a note which Lincoln wrote to the secretary of war:

"SEC. OF WAR.

"Please see this Pittsburgh boy. He is very young and I shall be satisfied with whatever you do with him.

"A. LINCOLN."

"August 21, 1863."

The "Pittsburgh boy" had joined the army when only seventeen. He had endured a long, tedious fever. He desired a furlough, and with a curious belief that he could get anything of advantage to himself if he could only see the President, he made his way into the White House one day, and the note above was the outcome of his interview.

Another incident shows his personal relations with one of the young soldiers, who was found asleep while on sentinel duty. This boy, William Scott by name, was from Vermont. He was tried by court-martial, and sentenced to be shot. The captain and members of his company, who were neighbors of his before they enlisted, begged that his life might be spared. But it was without avail. Then an appeal was made to Lincoln, who as usual was touched by it. The young Vermonter said that he had been brought up on a farm, and then went on to tell about the simple life he had lived there. He showed Lincoln the picture of his mother. He said, in telling the story of the interview to a comrade afterward, that he was just going to request Mr. Lincoln "to fix it so that the firing-party [which was to shoot him] would not be from our regiment," when he said: "My boy, you are not going to be shot to-morrow. . . . I am going to send you back to your regiment. But I have been put to a good deal of trouble on your account, . . . and what I want to know is, how you are going to pay my bill?"

The young soldier, in answer, spoke of various ways in which he could raise money for this purpose.

"Then," continued young Scott, in telling the story, "Mr. Lincoln put his hands on my shoulders and looked into my face as if he was sorry, and said: 'My boy, my bill is a very large one. Your friends cannot pay it, nor your bounty, nor your farm, nor all your comrades. There is only one man in all the world who can pay it, and his name is William Scott! If from this day William Scott does his duty, so that if I was there when he comes to die, he can look me in the face as he does now, and say, I have kept my promise, and I have done my duty as a soldier, then my debt will be paid. Will you make that promise and try to keep it?'

"I said I would make the promise, and with God's help I would keep it. I could say no more. I wanted to tell him how hard I would try to do all he wanted; but the words would not come, so that I had to let it all go unsaid. He went away out of my sight forever. I know I shall never see him again; but may God forget me if I forget his kind words or my promise."

Some months later he was in a charge made upon the Confederates in the Peninsular Campaign. His company had to go across a river, but was driven back with heavy loss, many wounded being left behind. The boy was among those who went back to rescue the fallen, and in doing so swam across the river again and again, each time returning with a wounded comrade. When he was bringing back his last living burden, a ball struck him in the breast and he fell with a mortal wound. He had paid in full the price that his commander-in-chief had asked for his release.

But far beyond the battle-fields and the hospitals, even in the stricken homes, Lincoln ministered to those who mourned. Among the bereaved women of the war was Mrs. Lydia Bixby, a poor working woman in Massachusetts and a widow, who, Lincoln heard, had lost five sons on the

A Fort on the Potomac River.

battle-field, and he wrote her the following beautiful letter of sympathy:

"I feel how weak and fruitless must be any word of mine which could attempt to beguile you from the grief of a loss so overwhelming, but I cannot refrain from tendering to you the consolation that may be found in the thanks of the Republic they died to save.

"I pray our Heavenly Father may assuage the anguish of your bereavement, and leave only the cherished memory of the loved and lost, and the solemn pride which must be yours to have laid so costly a sacrifice upon the altar of freedom."

The time Lincoln spent in listening to the pleadings by friends, in behalf of deserters who had been condemned to death, was large. It mattered not how busy he was. In the midst of the most perplexing situations he would· take time for a careful consideration of every case that was brought to his notice. Nothing gave him keener satisfaction than to prevent an injustice, or to lighten the burden of sorrow for some suffering soul. His usual telegram was: "Suspend execution and forward record for examination." But at times he sent the message: "Suspend execution of the death sentence until further orders."

"But," said a heart-stricken father on one occasion, "that does not pardon my boy."

"My dear man," responded the President, in a voice of gentleness and sympathy, while he laid his hand upon the father's shoulder, "do you suppose *I* will ever give orders for your boy's execution?"

So anxious was Lincoln that such orders for suspension of execution should promptly reach their destination, that he frequently went in person to the telegraph-office, even as late as midnight, and sent the telegram himself.

Even regard for good discipline could not make him deaf to the cry of age or helplessness in distress. When the President was told that the pardoning of so many wrong-doers was demoralizing the army, his prompt reply was: "But I need it. When I am worn and weary I can go to bed happy and sleep soundly after such an act. It rests me."

He could not bear to think of the execution of a very young soldier. He could not sleep if he knew that such an one was to be put to death on the following day. In one case he excused himself for suspending sentence of death by declaring, "His mother says he is but seventeen," and he pardoned the boy "on account of his tender age."

At another time he sent the following telegram to General Meade: "I am unwilling for any boy under eighteen to be shot."

Do you wonder that the soldiers loved President Lincoln? That their glowing admiration followed his towering figure when he honored them with a visit to the camp? And in making friends of these "Boys in Blue," he won his way to the hearts of thousands of fathers and mothers throughout the North who had good reason to bless the name and the memory of Abraham Lincoln.

There is no doubt that in his watchful care of the soldiers Lincoln was laying the foundation of undying loyalty in countless homes throughout the Union; for he was a man of the people, and when the time came for them to speak they knew him in whom they had put their trust.

CHAPTER XIII

RE-ELECTION OF LINCOLN

ALTHOUGH the tide of war had turned at Gettysburg, the crisis was not marked, as Lincoln had wished, by an emphatic wreckage of Confederate hopes. He had watched with earnest longing to see the retreating army so overwhelmed that they would be unable ever again to mass their forces for another encounter. But, as we have told elsewhere, Meade disappointed his chief and let Lee retreat safely into Virginia.

You remember how sorely disappointed and exasperated the President had been at another escape of the enemy after the battle of Antietam—an escape which seemed to him needless—and how disheartened he became in his long, vain search for a responsible general to lead the Union armies. But, as one of his admirers said, "Lincoln always had a card up his sleeve"; and just now, even in this crushing disappointment, he was not without resource. Vicksburg, you remember, had fallen the day following the battle of Gettysburg, and the President had been watching, with keen interest, the military progress of its hero, General Ulysses S. Grant.

As this resolute commander pushed his campaign down the river, never resting until victory was won, he held as

Lincoln in 1864.
From "Hannibal Hamlin," by C. E. Hamlin.

223

a magnet the anxious attention of the President; for here
was a man after his own heart. The modest general was
too busy achieving to send full reports of all he was doing.
Lincoln said of him, a few weeks after the capture of Vicksburg: "General Grant is a copious worker and fighter,
but a very meagre writer and telegrapher." But the President found a way to get news of what he wanted to know;
and it was not many weeks before he believed he had found
the right man, in the silent, aggressive hero of Vicksburg.

Grant had first recommended himself to the thoughtful
notice of the President at the time of the capture of Forts
Henry and Donelson, in February, 1862, by his reply to the
Confederate commander of Fort Donelson, who had asked
for terms of surrender. Grant had promptly sent back
the answer: "No terms except unconditional and immediate surrender can be accepted. I propose to move immediately on your works." The fort was surrendered with
fifteen thousand men. This terse message must have been
a refreshing draught to the commander-in-chief, at that
time wearied and harassed in his vain prodding of the
overcautious McClellan. He showed his appreciation by
appointing Grant major-general.

In the train of success followed petty jealousies, and
reports came to the President of Grant's unfitness for his
position, his enemies accusing him of intemperate habits.
Unshaken in his confidence, Lincoln replied to his informers:
"Tell me the brand of his whiskey and I will send it

General Ulysses S Grant.

to my other generals"; and to another he said: "This man fights. I can't spare him."

In November, 1863, after the capture of Vicksburg, by brilliant strategy Grant overwhelmingly defeated Bragg at Chattanooga. These achievements had so definitely marked him for promotion that Lincoln sent for him in the early spring of 1864 to come to Washington, where he received the appointment of lieutenant-general, giving him command, under the direction of the President, of all the Union armies.

On March 9, 1864, the President formally presented his commission with these words:

"General Grant, the nation's appreciation of what you have done, and its reliance upon you for what remains to do in the existing great struggle, are now presented, with this commission, constituting you lieutenant-general in the army of the United States. With this high honor devolves upon you, also, a corresponding responsibility. As the country trusts you, so, under God, it will sustain you. I scarcely need to add that with what I here speak for the nation goes my own hearty personal concurrence."

General Grant replied: "Mr. President, I accept with gratitude this commission for the high honor conferred. With the aid of the noble armies that have fought on so many fields for our common country, it will be my earnest endeavor not to disappoint your expectations. I feel the full weight of the responsibilities now devolving on me;

and know that if they are met, it will be due to those armies, and above all to the favor of that Providence which leads both nations and men."

In accordance with the wishes of the President, Grant was not only to have the entire military conduct of the war, but also the personal control of the Virginia campaign against Lee. It is understood that before accepting his appointment, Grant insisted that he must not be interfered with in his military duties. However that may be, we know he was left free to carry out his own plans in his own way. Lincoln himself offered suggestions but never gave orders. Having found the man upon whose ability and judgment he relied, he was willing to trust him.

We get some insight into the relations between the two men from the notes they exchanged just before the opening of the campaign, when Grant was about to advance against Lee's army, early in May.

The President's frank note ran as follows: "Not expecting to see you again before the spring campaign opens, I wish to express in this way my entire satisfaction with what you have done up to this time, so far as I understand it. The particulars of your plan I neither know nor seek to know. You are vigilant and self-reliant, and, pleased with this, I wish not to obtrude any constraints or restraints upon you. While I am very anxious that any great disaster or capture of our men in great numbers shall be avoided, I know these points are less likely to escape your attention than they would be mine. If there is anything wanting which is within my power to give, do not fail to let me know it. And now, with a brave army and a just cause, may God sustain you."

General Grant made answer: "From my first entrance into the volunteer service of the country to the present day, I have never had cause of complaint—have never expressed or implied a complaint against the administration, or the secretary of war, for throwing embarrassment in the way of my vigorously prosecuting what appeared to be my duty. Indeed, since the promotion which placed me in command of all the armies, and in view of the great responsibility and importance of success, I have been astonished at the readiness with which everything asked for has been yielded, without even an explanation being asked. Should my success be less than I desire and expect, the least I can say is, the fault is not yours."

These two notes reveal a mutual understanding between Grant and Lincoln that was most valuable in the conduct of the war. They were both simple, direct, honest, and straightforward, and each respected the good qualities of the other. It must therefore have been with confidence and keen satisfaction that Lincoln now looked forward to the outcome of the campaign as Grant's army started south toward Richmond.

This was the first time since the opening of the war that Lincoln felt released from the necessity of himself aiding in the work of planning and directing military movements. For now he had not only a lieutenant-general who held the full measure of his confidence, but also tried and trusted generals in subordinate fields. Next to

General William T. Sherman.

Grant, General William Tecumseh Sherman, who was to lead the army in the West, was the most conspicuous for his military successes. There were also the dashing young cavalry leader, General Philip H. Sheridan ("Phil" Sheridan, as his admirers liked to call him), who won the brilliant victory at Cedar Creek; and General George H.

Thomas, well-known as the "Rock of Chickamauga" because of his stubborn defense in that battle.

Meantime Lincoln's political problems were pressing, and were affecting his prospects of re-election. It was

his earnest desire to carry to a successful finish the work of the war. His friends knew that he wished the nomination, but there was opposition from many quarters. With that unselfishness that was always present with him, he said to Thurlow Weed: "Is there any man in the Democratic party who can push this war one step farther or faster

General Philip H. Sheridan.

than I? Because if there is, I want him to take my place." It is not necessary to go into details about all the complaints that were made; although, as we are to see later, a fruitful cause of much of the censure and abuse was the draft.

All through the dreary, dragging months of the war

there had been continuous unfavorable criticism. When generals disappointed and battles went wrong, the dissatisfaction and anger of all parties were heaped upon Lincoln. He was called inefficient, weak, irresolute. Murmurs and reproaches came from all directions and centred on him.

One of the most influential leaders working against him was Horace Greeley. And at this time he was favoring the choice of one of Lincoln's generals to succeed him. But the general was loyal to Lincoln.

General George H. Thomas.

In Lincoln's own official family was one who aspired to the Presidency, even though he would be supplanting his chief, and he was silently working to that end. This was Salmon P. Chase, secretary of the treasury. Although Lincoln knew of his personal disloyalty, he still held him in office because he was a faithful servant.

Another possible rival gave Lincoln more uneasiness, for he felt the man's worth and knew that his success was occasioning wide-spread enthusiasm. This was General Grant. But Grant was thoroughly devoted to Lincoln, and said to those who approached him on the subject tnat he would not accept the nomination if it was offered to him.

Through State Legislatures and caucuses, however, the people, more sagacious than their political leaders, were demanding Lincoln. They had confidence in him, because he had taken pains that they should understand him. His letters in answer to public criticism had been a powerful means of acquainting the public with his policy, for they were always so frank and so clearly and simply expressed that they were very convincing.

His stories and maxims, too, went much further than studied arguments. One of his sayings, "Never swap horses while crossing a stream," was repeated by the newspapers all over the country. It appealed to the people's sense of humor by its quaintness, and was most helpfully applied at this time to the changing of Presidents during the war. Lincoln's stories often contained the strongest arguments. Underlying them was the convincing truth that goes with solid reasoning. He used a story not only to clinch a point, but to put a situation in a concrete way, and often by a touch of humor to avert hard feeling. It has well been said that many of his stories contained the wisdom of ancient parables.

But in his story-telling Lincoln was often misunderstood, especially by those who were lacking in a sense of humor themselves. A good example of this appears in the following incident. On one occasion, when a Congressman came to the White House to present to the President a serious complaint, Lincoln began to tell a story. The man made an indignant protest. Lincoln, deeply pained, said with feeling: "I have great confidence in you, and great respect for you, and I know how sincere you are; but if I couldn't tell these stories, I should die." This simple statement changed the Congressman's indignation into sincere sympathy for President Lincoln.

Though it was declared that not one Republican in ten of the more earnest members of the Senate favored Lincoln, and though the speaker of the House said that Lincoln had but one strong political friend in the House, yet when the Republican National Convention met early in June, he received a renomination by an overwhelming majority on the first ballot—a strong proof that the people were heart and soul with the President.

In the meanwhile, what of campaigns and battles? A few words will explain the military situation in the summer of 1864. Early in May, as you will recall, Grant began his campaign against Lee in Virginia. When he crossed the Rapidan and entered the Wilderness, every foot of his advance was hotly contested by Lee's army. The fighting was terrible, and the Union losses enormous; but with unyielding determination Grant pressed on, writing to the President his stubborn resolve: "I propose to fight it out on this line if it takes all summer." It did take all summer and more, for Grant found it impossible to capture Richmond by attacking it on the north side. He therefore transferred his army across the James River and attacked the city from the south.

But at the end of the summer Lee still held on. The Union losses were something like sixty thousand. Some said: "Grant is failing." Many bitterly censured Lincoln also. They declared, with emphasis: "He is not strong enough for his task; he is lacking in practical talent."

Still the bloody fighting went on, and Lee managed his army with such skill and his men fought with such bravery that Grant made only slow progress. The Confederates still held Richmond.

It was a period of bitter disappointment and discouragement for those who were loyal to the Union cause. The hostile critics declared, as they had been doing for many months, that the military policy of the administration was a failure; that the war had been dragging on year after year with an enormous waste of material goods and human life; and that it was dragging on because the President was weak as an executive.

Their attitude seemed to be justified because neither Grant nor Sherman had, up to the last of August, 1864, done anything which the country looked upon as noteworthy. To be sure, Grant had advanced toward Richmond; but he had not captured the city, nor did it look as though he would capture it. Likewise, Sherman had made a steady advance toward Atlanta, but he had not captured Atlanta.

In fact, the summer of 1864 was a dark one for the people of the North. In the midst of the constantly increasing gloom over the failure of the Union armies a meeting of the National Executive Committee of the Republican party was held in New York City. After the meeting the chairman of the committee, Henry J. Raymond, who was editor of the *New York Times* and a loyal supporter of the administration, wrote to Mr. Lincoln as follows: "I am in active correspondence with your stanchest friends in every State, and from them all I hear but one report. The tide is setting strongly against us." For this unfortunate state of affairs he gave two reasons: (1) "the want of military success, and (2) the impression in some minds, and the fear and suspicion in others that we are not to have peace in any event under this administration, until slavery is abandoned. In some way or other the suspicion is widely diffused that we can have peace with Union if we would."

It was August 23, the day on which this letter probably reached President Lincoln, that he wrote upon a piece of paper the following memorandum:

"EXECUTIVE MANSION,
"WASHINGTON, August 23, 1864.

"This morning, as for some days past, it seems exceedingly probable that this administration will not be re-

elected. Then it will be my duty to so co-operate with
the President-elect as to save the Union between the election and the inauguration, as he will have secured his election on such ground that he cannot possibly save it afterward.

"A. LINCOLN."

When his Cabinet met he handed the folded paper to
all the members, who signed their names on the outside
without knowing what he had written.

Lincoln's action in this case was characteristic. He
always wished to keep faith with his better self. He was
always troubled until he had decided, after carefully weighing all the facts involved, just what it was right for him to
do. But when he had reached his decision, nothing could
turn him from his purpose.

Six days after Lincoln wrote the memorandum mentioned above, something occurred which caused much
anxious thought on the part of Mr. Lincoln's friends. This
was the meeting in Chicago of the Democratic National
Convention. There were two strong factions present—the
"War Democrats," and the "Peace Democrats." The
latter was powerful enough to force into the platform, although in the face of stubborn and even bitter opposition,
a peace plank. This declared that "after four years of
failure to restore the Union by the experiment of war, justice, humanity, liberty, and the public welfare demand"

that an immediate effort be made to stop the fighting on the battlefield, and to call a convention of the States with the purpose of restoring peace "at the earliest practicable moment" "on the basis of the Federal Union of the States."

To the extent of getting this peace plank into the platform, then, the "Peace Democrats" scored a point. But the "War Democrats" had a greater success, for they brought about the nomination of their favorite candidate, General McClellan. He accepted the nomination, but in his letter of acceptance he expressly repudiated the so-called peace plank.

Amid all this political doubt and fear the President never wavered. He was determined, above all else and at whatever cost, to save the Union. The cost would surely be heavy, both in money and men. But he would save it even if he had to resort to another draft; or, as his enemies said, to act the part of a military dictator by authorizing arbitrary arrests of people who criticised the government, or by stopping for a time the publication of hostile newspapers. His present unpopularity with this group of critics was due to his already having resorted to such measures, and especially to the draft. To make this clear, let us go back a little.

When the war broke out, more volunteers offered their services than were thought necessary. But before the end of the second year, the war had grown so unpopular or doubtful of result that volunteering had almost entirely ceased. So few battles had been won by Union armies that men lost heart; and besides, nearly all the young men without families to support had already gone into the war, so that volunteering, now, meant a severe sacrifice.

To meet the serious situation, Congress passed a Conscription Act in March, 1863. The draft itself, which affected all able-bodied male citizens between eighteen and forty-five years of age, was begun in the early part of the following summer. The result in New York City was a terrible riot lasting four days. Before it could be brought under military control the mob, in its savage madness and fury, had destroyed property to the value of one million five hundred thousand dollars, and something like one thousand people had been killed or wounded, many of whom were negroes. Governor Seymour, of New York State, urged President Lincoln to suspend the draft. But Mr. Lincoln wisely refused; the necessity was imperative.

Moreover, in 1864 he ordered further drafts, simply because he saw no other way to supply the Union armies with much-needed men. One of these drafts, which was for five hundred thousand men, was ordered by Lincoln to take place in September. The shocking losses on the battle-field, especially in Grant's army in Virginia, had so depleted the Union armies that more men were absolutely necessary. Knowing that this draft was so odious to the people that it might injure Lincoln's chances of election, some of his friends urged him to suspend it until after election day. But he was not the man to think of his own interests if they interfered with the interests of the coun-

Draft Riot in New York City.

try. So he persisted in issuing the draft, although in so doing he knew he was risking his own re-election.

In the midst of the uncertainty and discouragement of

the hour, suddenly the sunlight broke through the clouds, for in August Farragut destroyed the forts in Mobile Bay, and cut off the city from the outside world; in September Sherman captured Atlanta; and in October Sheridan, in a series of crushing victories, cleared the Shenandoah Valley of the enemy. These victories were most timely. They not only changed the military outlook, but they assured Lincoln's success at the polls, early in November. Out of a total of two hundred and thirty-two presidential electors chosen, two hundred and eleven favored Lincoln. It was a splendid indorsement by the people, and gave him the longed-for opportunity to finish his work.

As we should expect, he accepted the well-earned tribute in a truly modest spirit. When on the night following his election he reached the White House (about two o'clock in the morning), he found a party of serenaders waiting for a speech. With characteristic honesty and simplicity, he said to them: "My friends, if I know my heart, my gratitude is free from any intent of personal triumph. I do not impugn the motive of any one who opposed me. It is no pleasure for me to triumph over any one, but I give thanks to the Almighty for this evidence of the people's resolution to stand by free government and the rights of humanity."

CHAPTER XIV

LAST DAYS OF A GREAT LIFE

THE second inauguration of Lincoln took place without unusual incident on March 4, 1865. The event is marked especially by the beauty of his inaugural address, which is known as the Second Inaugural. This was one of the noblest State papers ever written, and in its tenderness almost prophetic. Passing lightly over the matter of his policies, which, he said, were too well known to be discussed, he closed with a passage that has come to be regarded as a classic of our language. The words fell like a benediction upon those who heard them. They were like the parting counsel of a father spoken to those he loves, and proved to be in reality a farewell to the American people:

"With malice toward none; with charity for all; with firmness in the right, as God gives us to see the right—let us strive on to finish the work we are in; to bind up the nation's wounds; to care for him who shall have borne the battle, and for his widow and his orphan; to do all which may achieve and cherish a just and lasting peace among ourselves and with all nations."

The message reveals clearly the depth and strength of Lincoln's religious nature, which is traceable in all the crises

of his life. It harks back to the early days, when his soul
was attuned to nature and God in the vast solitudes of the
wilderness. There we can see him as a little lad kneeling
with his mother and sister at a small grave in the Kentucky
woodland. Again, in the Indiana clearing we see him at

Lincoln's Second Inauguration, March 4, 1865.

the bedside of that dying Christian mother, and feel that
his spirit is answering back to hers as the door opens for
her on the eternal mysteries and she bids her son good-by.

Along through the years of his early manhood, in all
his relations of life, private and public, there is evident a
deep and constant sense of duty and of trust in a higher
power. This abiding faith is most clearly manifested in the
stormy, tempestuous years of his life in the White House.

Lincoln in 1865.
From a photograph by Brady.

When he entered upon his duties as President, it seemed to the world that our nation was intrusting her destiny to an uncertain pilot in a frail bark. Even his friends were fearful. But in Lincoln's soul there was no doubt. His farewell words to his friends and neighbors on that chilly February morning in 1861, "Without the assistance of that Divine Being . . . I cannot succeed; with that assistance, I cannot fail," show the source of the strength and calmness which never forsook him.

As defeat followed defeat, and one disaster crowded upon another in the early days of the war, his faith and courage never wavered. In one of the darkest hours, when the Merrimac threatened to destroy the Union fleet and the country was in panic, we hear the clear, calm voice of Lincoln declaring: "I have not the slightest fear of any result which shall fatally impair our military and naval strength. This is God's fight, and he will win in his own good time. He will take care our enemies do not press us too far." At another time he said: "I have been driven to my knees many times by the overwhelming conviction that I have nowhere else to go."

The week after the battle of Gettysburg, General Sickles, who had been in the battle, asked Mr. Lincoln if he had not been anxious during the Gettysburg campaign.

Mr. Lincoln replied: "I had no fear."

"How could that be?" asked the general.

"In the pinch of your campaign up there," replied Lincoln, "when everybody seemed panic-stricken and nobody could tell what was going to happen, I went into my room one day and locked the door, and got down on my knees before Almighty God and prayed to him mightily for a victory at Gettysburg. I told God that if we were to win the battle he must do it, for I had done all I could. I told him this was his war, and our cause was his cause, but that we couldn't stand another Fredericksburg or Chancellorsville. And then and there I made a solemn vow to Almighty God that if he would stand by our boys at Gettysburg I would stand by him. And he did, and I will. And after that—I don't know how it was, and I can't explain it—but soon a sweet comfort crept into my soul that things would go all right at Gettysburg, and that is why I had no fears about you."

It has been well said that Lincoln lived in the spirit. Of creeds and dogmas he was no lover. He said: "Whenever any church will inscribe over its altar as a qualification of membership the Saviour's statement of the substance of the law and gospel, 'Thou shalt love the Lord thy God with all thy heart, and with all thy soul, and with all thy mind, and thy neighbor as thyself,' that church will I join with all my heart and soul."

Holding firmly to the belief that, if we do right, God will be with us, and if God is with us we cannot fail, it was a sore trial and perplexity to him that the Union cause was so slow in winning. He believed it was a righteous cause, and yet God did not bring victory to the Union armies. After pondering long, he reached the conclusion that the Civil War was a punishment to the American people, both North and South, for the crime of enslaving the negroes. This belief is clearly set forth in the Second Inaugural, in which he says: "The Almighty has his own purposes. . . . If we shall suppose that American slavery is one of those offenses which, in the providence of God, must needs come . . . and that he gives to both North and South this terrible war as the woe due to those by whom the offense came, shall we discern therein any departure from those divine attributes which the believers in a living God ascribe to him? Fondly do we hope . . . that this mighty scourge of war may speedily pass away. Yet, if God wills that it continue until all the wealth piled by the bondman's two hundred and fifty years of unrequited toil shall be sunk, and until every drop of blood drawn with the lash shall be paid by another drawn with the sword, as said three thousand years ago, so still it must be said: 'The judgments of the Lord are true and righteous altogether.' "

In less than a month after Lincoln's second inauguration Grant had succeeded in forcing Lee out of Richmond (April 2). Lee then retreated westward with the purpose of joining General Johnston, who was moving toward him from the south. But Grant followed closely to catch up with Lee before the two armies could unite; and it seemed inevitable that Lee's surrender must come soon.

In anticipation of this important event, concerning which it seemed desirable that he should have personal conferences with the commanding general, late in March Lincoln visited Grant's headquarters at City Point, on the James River. Soon after his arrival Mrs. Lincoln and Tad joined him, and his son Robert came from Harvard to ex-

Landing Supplies at City Point.

perience something of the soldier's life as a member of Grant's staff.

During his stay Lincoln often rode with Grant miles and miles over the corduroy roads of the swamps, while at night he sat by the camp-fire and exchanged stories with the officers. Believing that the long period of fighting was near its close, he seemed to enjoy a sense of freedom from the nerve-wearing anxiety of the White House.

On hearing of Lee's retreat he said: "I must see Richmond." When he reached the city he found disorder, confusion, and chaos everywhere. Although he knew that his life was in danger in the Confederate capital, he walked, for a mile and a half through the streets, leading Tad by the hand, with no guard except ten marines.

As he passed along, the negroes crowded about him in their eagerness to touch his garments. Some with tears of gratitude fell upon their knees at his feet, as in worship. But he said, "Do not kneel to me; that is not right"; and then, gently: "God bless you, and let me pass on."

When the party entered the building which was used as Union headquarters, and which had been also the official residence of the Confederate President, some one remarked to Lincoln: "Jefferson Davis ought to be hanged." The forbearing President promptly responded: "Judge not, that ye be not judged." When, a few days later, Mrs. Lincoln remarked to a friend that the national capital was "filled with our enemies," the President, hearing her words, raised his arm and with a lack of his usual gentleness and patience, retorted: "Enemies! We must never speak of that." Even in the hour of victory he harbored no bitterness against any human being, and was strongly opposed to harsh measures against the Confederate leaders.

This is plainly indicated in his plan to restore peaceful relations between the warring sections of the Union with as little friction as possible. In his plan of reconstruction,

Lincoln Visiting Richmond.

which he had been for many months forecasting, he displayed not only freedom from "malice" toward the Confederate States, but also his exceptional and marked prac-

tical common sense. "We all agree," he declared, "that the seceded States, so-called, are out of their proper practical relation with the Union, and that the sole object of the government, civil and military, in regard to these States, is to again get them into the proper practical relation. I believe that it is not only possible, but in fact easier to do this without deciding or even considering whether these States have ever been out of the Union than with it. Finding themselves safely at home, it would be utterly immaterial whether they have ever been abroad."

But Lincoln could not wait at City Point for the final act in the great campaign, being called back to Washington by an accident to Secretary Seward. By the time he reached Washington, however, Lee had surrendered (April 9), and the capital was already rejoicing.

Everywhere in the North there was unbounded enthusiasm, for Lee's surrender meant that the war was practically at an end. But to no one could it mean so much as to the worn and harassed President. The strain of the load he had carried during the terrible years of the war was written in the unspeakable sadness of his countenance. On one occasion he said, in weariness of spirit, "I feel as though I shall never be glad any more"; on another he remarked, with his whimsical smile: "I wish George Washington or some other old patriot were here to take my place for a while, so that I could have a little rest."

But after it became certain that the war would end in

favor of the Union, there came a marked change in his looks and ways. His face brightened, and he began to appear more like the light-hearted Lincoln of former days. Again, also, he took a special interest in all that suggested peace and repose. He enjoyed reading over and over poems that spoke of things serene and peaceful. He liked to linger in quiet spots.

Many years later Mrs. Lincoln told the following incident, which took place while they were still at Grant's headquarters in Virginia: They were driving one day along the James River and came to a country cemetery. It was a quiet, shaded spot.

General Grant and Mrs. Grant with their Son at City Point, Va.

They got out of their carriage and walked among the graves, Mr. Lincoln looking serious and thoughtful. In a few moments he said to his wife: "Mary, you are younger than I. You will survive me. When I am gone, lay my remains in some quiet spot like this."

Again in Washington, the President at once set in motion the formal business of closing the war.   His first measure was an order suspending the draft, and this was published in the newspapers of Friday morning, April 14.

Great joy spread like a tidal wave over the country. The cry, "Lee has surrendered—the war is over!" was repeated again and again.   It broke on every town, village, and wayside settlement until it seemed as if the winds of heaven had taken it up and tossed it back and forth. Perils and hardships and all the black evil of war were for the time forgotten.   In countless homes mothers wept and laughed in turn, as they thought of the home-coming of their boys.   Even those who had lost their dear ones were glad that the turmoil would soon end, and that they had not sacrificed their treasure in vain.   Bells were rung, flags were unfurled, and the national colors, decorating buildings and waving from flagstaffs on every side, never appeared more beautiful.

It was a happy people that gave welcome to this Good Friday of April 14, 1865.   The day, usually observed by many with fasting and prayer, was on this occasion filled with a spirit of profound thanksgiving.   Spring and hope were in the warm sunshine and balmy air, while budding trees and blooming flowers symbolized the joy that was blossoming again in human hearts.   Nothing gave hint of the awful tragedy that was so soon to bring gloom to the country.

Grant had arrived in Washington that morning to be present at the Cabinet meeting, held as usual on Friday. Many questions were asked regarding the safety of General Sherman, for it was thought that he was on the point of meeting in battle with General Johnston somewhere in the Carolinas. Several of the Cabinet were anxious about the situation, but Lincoln was not. He said he was sure that good news would come from that quarter, because he had dreamed the night before the same dream that had come to him several times on the eve of great battles. It had preceded the battles of Murfreesboro, Antietam, Gettysburg, and Vicksburg. He had no doubt that a battle had taken place, or soon would take place, and he went on: "Johnston will be beaten, for I had this strange dream again last night. It must relate to Sherman; my thoughts are in that direction and I know of *no other very important event which is likely just now to occur.*" Fateful dream! It was the forerunner of a catastrophe greater than any battle of the war.

The day was a happy one for Mr. Lincoln. Captain Robert Lincoln was home from service under General Grant, and father and son had an hour's talk over the campaign. That afternoon the President and his wife took a long drive. His mood was very cheerful and tender. While they were out together he said: "Mary, we have had a hard time of it since we came to Washington; but the war is over, and with God's blessing we may hope for four years of peace and happiness, and then we will go back to Illinois, and pass the rest of our lives in quiet. I will open a law office at Springfield or Chicago, and practise law, and at least do enough to help give us a livelihood."

Never had Lincoln seemed in happier spirit than on this day of great triumph. His heart was filled with gratitude to God, and overflowed in love and kindness to his fellow men.

We like to dwell on this brief period of his life, when the heavy burdens of the war lifted, and the joy of achieved purpose reflected itself in his lightened countenance and cheerful bearing. Stanton said of him: "I never saw him so happy." But his wife, more apprehensive, said: "I never saw you like this except before our dear Willie died.''

Mrs. Lincoln's illusive foreboding soon gave place to shocking reality. She had arranged a theatre-party for that evening at Ford's Theatre, in honor of General and Mrs. Grant, who were guests at the White House. The papers had announced that they were to occupy a box. But, as General and Mrs. Grant decided to go North, Miss Harris and Major Rathbun, daughter and stepson of Senator Ira Harris, were invited to take their places. When evening came, Lincoln seemed loath to go, but he said: "The people will be disappointed," and so the plan was carried out.

The President's party did not reach the theatre until after the play, "The American Cousin," had begun. When

The Last Portrait of Lincoln.

From a photograph by Alexander Gardner.   Copyright by Watson Porter.

they entered, the band struck up "Hail to the Chief." There was great enthusiasm. The audience cheered, the men waved their hats and the women their handkerchiefs, the action of the play being suspended meanwhile. The party in the box laid aside their wraps and turned, smiling and bowing, as they took their seats.

During the play Mr. Lincoln, who occupied an armchair near the railing in plain sight of the audience, chatted in a genial way with the members of his party, and laughed with the audience at the flashes of humor in the dialogue.

During the third act, had the audience been watching, they might have observed a dark, handsome young man going along the corridor and entering the passage which led to the President's box. It was the actor, John Wilkes Booth, an extreme secessionist, excited by hate at the downfall of his cause. Having entered, he closed the door and fastened it so that it could not be opened from the outside. Then stealthily entering the box, he took deliberate aim and shot the President in the back of the head.

Major Rathbun at once grappled with the assassin, and received a deep and wide wound in his arm from the knife Booth carried in his left hand. The murderer, tearing himself away, leaped from the box to the stage. In so doing he caught the spur of his left foot in the silken flag draping the box, and fell so heavily that he broke his leg. But he was able to get to his feet, and, limping across the stage, he faced the audience and shouted: "Sic semper tyrannis!"

("Thus be it always to tyrants!") Then, before any one could reach him, he rushed through a familiar exit to the street, where a horse awaited him.

The audience was at first startled, then stunned, as it realized what had happened. The shot—a woman's cry— a cloud of smoke—all had taken place in a moment of time. Major Rathbun's shout, "Stop him! He has shot the President!" roused them to the horror of the situation. Then in helpless rage and grief some rushed shouting to the stage in pursuit of the murderer—others ran to the box. Surgeons came, and the silent figure of the President was borne from the theatre to the street, and across the way to the nearest house.

There, in a small room, he was laid unconscious upon the bed. He lingered throughout the night, tenderly watched by those about him—his family, members of the Cabinet, and other friends. A little after seven the next morning he died. As he breathed his last Secretary Stanton, who had become Lincoln's devoted friend, said: "Now he belongs to the ages."

All night, while the spirit of the President was passing into the unseen, Washington had been in a ferment of confusion and horror. Messengers had been hurrying hither and yon, spreading the news and bearing orders from the secretary of war, who at once put the city under military control.

Next morning all the papers gave news of the tragedy.

The shock and horror of it spread everywhere. A pall of silence fell over the people, and they walked with bowed heads and whitened faces. In New York shops were closed. All business was suspended. The joy of yesterday was forgotten in the universal sorrow. Flags and bunting gave place to emblems of grief and mourning. From the Battery to the Park, public buildings and private dwellings were draped in black. Even the meanest hovel in the poorest quarter displayed some token, however simple, of sorrow for the death of the President. Similar signs of mourning were visible in all the great cities of the North, and in all the towns and villages. The general grief spread even to the remote farms. All classes, especially the plain people, felt that they had lost a friend.

On the following Wednesday, while funeral services were being held at twelve o'clock in the White House, business was suspended, and similar services were conducted in churches throughout the North. Thus in unison did the people of the nation pay their last formal tribute of devotion to the martyred President.

The next morning, the funeral train bearing the body of Abraham Lincoln to its last resting-place, near Springfield, Illinois, started on its sad journey of nearly two thousand miles. The route was almost the same as that by which, as President-elect, he had come to Washington a little more than four years before.

As the funeral cortège passed on its way there were

almost continuous demonstrations of sorrow.   In the large
centres the funeral train rested, the casket was borne through
the streets, and the body of the President lay in state, while

The National Lincoln Monument at Springfield, Illinois.

an innumerable throng gazed upon the face of their dead
hero.   Even at the smallest country stations the people, in
reverent silence, stood with bared heads and tear-filled eyes
as the funeral train moved by.   The silent dead passed between continuous walls of living people.   Day or night,

rain or shine, there was the same constant attendance, and the sombre emblems of mourning along the route were only less impressive than the crowds of grief-stricken people.

But the most tender of all the expressions of love and sorrow came from those who had been his friends and neighbors before he was called to the White House. As they looked upon his familiar face for the last time, they thought of him, not as the emancipator of the slaves, nor as President of the United States, but as one who in earlier years had been kind and helpful in a thousand ways.

Even though Lincoln has taken his place among the immortals, his memory still lives and his influence pervades the life of the nation whose leader he was. What it was in his great soul that enabled him, untutored and untrained in conventional ways, to control for four years the destiny of a great people, we may not understand. But we may recognize in his righteous purpose, his clear understanding, his wise judgment, his earnest efforts to do what was right, the means by which he reached his goal. With unflinching devotion he pushed resolutely forward, never changing, never swerving, when he believed he was in the right, no matter what ridicule or abuse was heaped upon his head. Many times he was cut to the quick by an ungrateful nation, or an unworthy follower; but to know his duty and to do it were his sole concern.

Although inflexible in the path of duty, he never failed

in his gentle forgiveness of those who wronged him, and in his sympathetic care of those who sought his help. He was a father to the soldiers, a friend to the widowed and the orphaned, and he yearned to enfold the nation in his protecting care.

He was so simple and modest in manner, that those with whom he walked did not realize his greatness. But when death suddenly removed him, the world by a quick instinct recognized him as one of the greatest of men. It beheld a conqueror who had led the nation through many perils, achieving his purpose and accomplishing his task. "With malice toward none, with charity for all," he had saved the Union and had freed the slaves.

INDEX

other trip to New Orleans, 35–38; witnesses a slave-auction, 38; goes to New Salem to manage Offutt's store, 38, 39; the wrestling-match with Jack Armstrong, 40; "Honest Abe," 41; studies English grammar, 42, 43; his kindness and generous spirit makes for him many friends, 43; goes to the Black Hawk War, 44–48; defeated for the legislature, 49; takes up store-keeping with Berry as partner, 50; finds a copy of Blackstone's "Commentaries," 51; appointed postmaster of New Salem, 52; he and his partner, failing, sell out their store, 51, 52; his honesty, 54; studies surveying, 54–56; burning desire to know things clearly and thoroughly, 56; his horse, saddle, and surveying instruments sold in payment of debts, 57; elected to the legislature, 57; falls in love with Ann Rutledge, 58–61; elected for a second term to the legislature, 61; receives license to practise law in autumn of 1836, 62; goes to Springfield in spring of 1837, 62–64; becomes a suitor of Miss Mary Todd, whom he marries in 1842, 66–68; in the State legislature for four successive terms—from 1834 to 1842, 68–70; elected to Congress, 70; his opposition to the Mexican War, 70–72; introduces a bill to abolish slavery in District of Columbia, 72; retires from politics and takes up again the practise of law, 73, 74; his law-office, 74; law practice on the circuit, 74, 75; his care and tenderness for helpless creatures, 75; his dress, 76; his good nature, 77; life at the taverns, 78; a favorite of Judge Davis, 79; his stories, 79, 80; his great power over a jury, 80; unable to argue against his convic-

tions, 81; the Armstrong case, 81–83; counsel for the Illinois Central Railroad and in a famous patent case, 83, 84; books and study once more a passion with him, 84–86; as a home-maker and host, 86; lives a simple, natural, industrious life, 87, 88; deeply stirred by the repeal of the Missouri Compromise in 1854, 89, 91; bitterly opposed to the extension of slavery into new States, 92; his remarkable speed in the Bloomington convention in 1856, 93, 94; his leadership in the Republican party in Illinois, 94; his house-divided-against-itself speech in 1858, 95, 96; challenges Senator Douglas to a series of debates, 96; the two debaters compared, 97, 98; the trying question he put to Douglas, 100, 101; incidents in the debates, 101–104; results of the debates, 104–106; the Cooper Union speech, 107–110; makes addresses in several New England cities, 110; his nomination for the presidency, 111–116; how the nomination was received, 116, 117; Lincoln and the nomination, 117; the formal notification, 117–119; the letter of acceptance, 119, 120; an enthusiastic campaign, 120, 121; his simple life during the campaign, 121–125; the excitement of the country over the slavery question, 123, 124; inflexible on the question of extending slavery into new States, 126–129; writes his inaugural address, 131; farewell visits to his mother and his law partner, 131, 133; farewell speech on leaving Springfield, 134, 135; his journey to Washington, 135–139; his speeches on the way, 136; inaugurated, 139–142; inaugural address, 141, 142; attitude toward Lincoln on his becom-

ing President, 143, 144; Lincoln
and his cabinet, 144–150; Lincoln
and Stanton, 146; Lincoln and
Seward, 148–150; Lincoln and Fort
Sumter, 150–153; declares the
South under blockade, 153; Lincoln and the "Trent Affair," 157–
159; Lincoln and his boys in the
White House, 159, 160; his love
for children, 161; Lincoln and Fré-
mont, 163; Lincoln and the border
States, 141, 142, 163, 164, 172, 173;
Lincoln and McClellan, 164–172;
Lincoln and Greeley, 176; good
feeling between him and the people, 177, 178; his critics hard on
him, 178, 179; a remarkable
cabinet meeting, 180–182; Lincoln
announces the Emancipation Proclamation on September 22, 1862,
183; he issues it on January 1,
1863, 185; he appoints McClellan
once more in command of the
troops around Washington, 188;
removes McClellan from command,
191; Lincoln and Burnside, 191,
192; Lincoln and Hooker, 193–
197; the finding of generals a perplexing problem, 197; Lincoln as a
military leader, 197; Lincoln and
General Meade, 199–202; the
Gettysburg address, 203–207; his
simplicity and friendliness, 208–
221; his simple habits, 208–210;
always ready to help those who
sought his aid, 210, 211; his sympathetic relations with the "Boys
in Blue," 211–221; Lincoln in the
hospitals, 214–216; how he saved
the life of William Scott, 217, 218;
his letter to Mrs. Bixby, 219; his
tenderness toward deserters, 220,
221; loyalty toward Lincoln, 221;
his relations with Grant, 222–228;
his attitude toward re-election, 230;
his critics, 231; his rivals, 231; his
stories, 232, 233; bitterly censured,

234; dark outlook for re-election,
235, 236; Lincoln and the draft,
237–239; Lincoln's re-election, 240;
his second inauguration, 241, 242;
his constant sense of duty and of
trust in a higher power, 242–246;
visits Grant's headquarters and
goes to Richmond, 247, 248; his
plan of reconstruction, 249, 250;
his heavy load during the war, 250;
his drive along the James River
with Mrs. Lincoln, 251; meets with
his cabinet on Good Friday, 253;
shot by J. Wilkes Booth, 254–256;
his death, 257; his body carried to
its final resting-place, 258–260; his
character and greatness, 260, 261

Lincoln, Mary Todd, 66, 138, 248, 251, 253, 254
Lincoln, Nancy Hanks, 1, 3, 13, 14
Lincoln, Robert Todd, 87, 250
Lincoln, Sarah, 20, 29
Lincoln, Sarah Bush Johnston, 14, 15
Lincoln, Thomas, 1–7, 14, 15, 19, 22, 29
Lincoln, Thomas ("Tad"), 87, 159–161
Lincoln, William Wallace, 87, 159–161

McClellan, George B., 83, 164–172, 188, 190, 191, 237
McDowell, Irvin, 156, 168, 170, 172
McNeil, John, 58, 59
Meade, George G., 199–202
Missouri Compromise, 89, 90

Nicolay, John G., 150

Pinkerton, Allan, 137
Polk, James K., 71
Popular sovereignty, 91

Raymond, Henry J., 235
Rutledge, Ann, 58–61

Scott, William, 217, 218
Scott, Winfield, 128, 151, 154